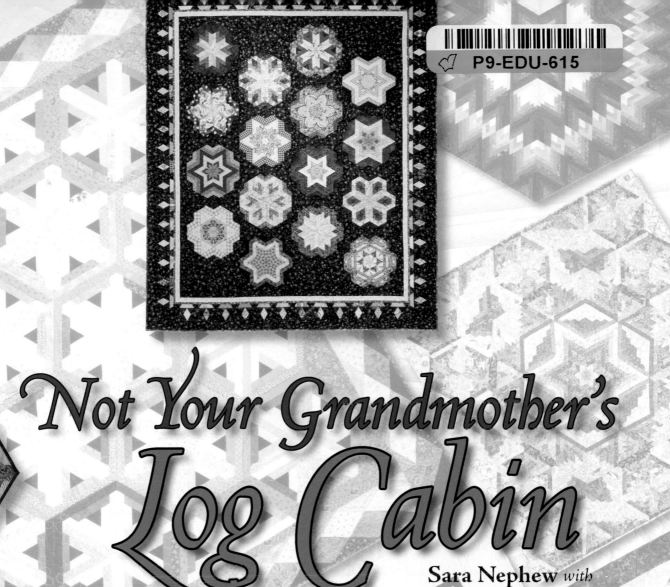

# Not Your Grandmother's Log Cabin

**Sara Nephew** *with*

**Marci Baker**

Clearview Triangle
©2008, Sara Nephew with Marci Baker
Editor: Marci Baker
Assistant Editor: Anita Hartinger
Production Coordinator: Susan Simono
Copy Editor: Kris Krischano
Graphic Design & Layout: Mark Talbot of Xplore Design, Inc.
www.xplore-design.com
Cover Design: Marci Baker/Mark Talbot
Photography by Randy Pfizenmaier of Fusebox Studios, except as noted
www.fuseboxstudio.com
Printing: Cedar Graphics, Hiawatha, IA
www.cedargraphicsinc.com

Published by Clearview Triangle, an imprint of Alicia's Attic, Inc.,
Fort Collins, CO
1-888-348-6653, 970-224-1336, fax 970-224-1362
www.aliciasattic.com, info@aliciasattic.com

Printed in the United States of America
ISBN: 978-1-930294-06-6
Library of Congress Control Number: 2008923480

Our goal is to provide you with complete instructions for an enjoyable quilting experience. Every effort has been made to ensure accurate information. The publisher assumes no liability for loss because of variation in materials, human error, varying personal ability, etc. If you do find an error or have a question, we would appreciate hearing from you. A list of changes will be available on our web site should any modifications be necessary.

On the front cover: foreground - Will O' Wisp quilt by Kathy Syring, in back – Fire Garden (Fireworks) by Scott Hansen, log home of Bill and Linda Butin, in Red Feather Lakes, CO.

On the back cover: upper left – close-up of Sunshine Came Softly (Frost Star) by Linda DeGaeta, lower left – Tropical Mandala (Badge of Honor) by Linda DeGaeta, upper right – Beauty of Africa by Sara Nephew, lower right – Fire Garden (Fireworks) by Scott Hansen

# Acknowledgements

With Thanks from Sara: The author is in awe at the generosity and demonstrated talent of all her very special pattern testers; Marci Baker, Joyce Lawrence Cambron, Diane Coombs, Bobbie Crosby, Linda DeGaeta, Joan Dawson, Janet Goad, Scott Hansen, Juliette Hawley, Janice Jamison, Kathie Kryla, Sarah Newman, Terri Shinn, Kathleen Springer, Kathy Syring, Linda Tellesbo, and Bonnie Walker. The beauty of their work adds hugely to the value of this book.

Marci Baker, in addition, helped produce this book as publisher, as emotional support, and as special assistant tester, technical editor, and creator of the charts for fabric requirements. We always have fun together. And thanks again to Kris Krischano, who reads it first for mistakes. I need all the help I can get!

With Thanks from Marci: Thank you to Susan Simono for her patience and organization, to Anita Hartinger for finding my words, to Mark Talbot for outstanding graphic design, and to Randy Pfizenmaier for making these quilts come to life in print. Many thanks to Bill and Linda Butin for their generosity in sharing their log home for the cover photo, especially during the holidays. Thank you to Dale Nephew for his heart-felt wisdom and sound advice throughout the project.

A special thank you to my husband, Clint, and sons, Kevin and Marcus, for their patience, understanding, and catering when I worked long hours. As co-author and editor of this project, I am appreciative of Sara's confidence and trust in my abilities to publish her incredible designs. She has given me an opportunity that has helped me grow and think outside of the box. Let's do this again with your next set of designs!

Special thanks to these manufacturers:
Maywood Studio
Windham Fabrics
Fabric Freedom
Benartex
Quilter's Dream Batting
Omnigrid

*Sara's Chrysanthemum piece fit right in with the Tatami room at the Butin log home. A perfect example of the elegance and variety possible with these log cabin designs.*

This book is dedicated to
our fun and exciting collaboration!

# Table of Contents

# Preface

For many years, when I have given my lecture "Quilts From the Clearview Triangle", which shows the many designs from all my books based on the equilateral triangle, I generally repeat to my audience that whatever you can do with squares, you can do with triangles. My husband has been listening to my lectures and he said, "Then you need to do 60° log cabin quilts."

Actually, I had done log cabin quilts many years ago. It is how I got into these quilt designs in the first place. I was a beginning quilter, with a small stash of fabric, having fun trying designs and making quilts for my family and friends out of corduroy and clothing scraps. I was also taking classes and reading books.

Two of our three children were approaching high school age, and looking ahead to college we could see that we would have two students in college at the same time. Where would the money come from? Well, what if I made quilts to sell? Making and selling is what I had done as a jeweler and cloisonné artist, so it came natural to me to consider it in my new interest – quilting.

I was playing with miniature (four-inch) log cabin blocks, having lots of fun, and many people were offering to buy the resulting wall hangings. So that's what I started to make to sell. I cut one-inch strips of cotton or wool, sewed them to a foundation of old sheeting to make the blocks, and arranged the blocks into the layout they looked best in. Eventually I made more than sixty of these wall hangings and sold most of them. By then I had baskets of one-inch strips sitting around, and was getting bored, trying to think of what else I could do with those strips that would be fun. In my library was a book by Jeffrey Gutcheon called "Diamond Patchwork" in which he showed how any quilt block could be drafted at a 60° angle, and the beautiful quilts his students made using this approach. So I decided to try a miniature log cabin 60° design, as shown here. I had some Plexiglas from a garage sale, and used my husband's band saw to make a template for the foundation pieces of old sheet. When I had to set the log cabin diamonds together, it was difficult to deal with the bulk of fabric, doing a set-in. I thought, "This would be so much easier if this was a triangle!" The proverbial light bulb came on in my head and the excitement began. I bought two 60° triangles from an office supply store, taped them together with clear packaging tape, and drew lines one inch apart from the base to the tip. The first Clearview Triangle ruler was born. I sewed strips together and used my ruler to cut triangles out and arrange them to make designs. It was so much fun!

*One of Sara's first quilting projects, a wall hanging with 60° log cabin blocks.*

Photo by Sara Nephew

I began learning how to work with fabric cut at a different angle, and experimenting with all the designs flowing from this new approach. Stars, floral looks, even isometric 3-D designs took shape on my graph paper. Soon I began to write pattern books full of those designs. Moving on from the log cabin quilts was easy.

Thanks to those first log cabin quilts I became an author and began to travel and teach. I even started a business manufacturing my own isometric rulers so everyone could easily try the techniques I was having fun with. Then Clearview Triangle became a publishing company too. Who could have imagined all this would happen?

Nineteen books and twenty-three years later, I am back at the beginning, working with log cabin quilts again. After years of designing isometric quilts and teaching classes, my skills have grown. Now I can design 60° log cabin quilts without set-ins and without so much bulk. Here is a book filled with dozens of new quilts. I hope you like them as much as I do!

Sara Nephew

# Introduction

Log cabin is a traditional pattern that most quilters have tried at one time or another. The idea is simple. Start in the middle of the block with a square (usually red - this is the chimney in the center of the cabin and the red is the fire). Then add concentric strips to the square until you have the size you want your block to be. The design of the block changes depending on the order in which you sew the strips. Popular variations of the log cabin block are Courthouse Steps and Pineapple. The design of the quilt changes depending how you arrange the blocks. Many different arrangements are possible.

If you change to a 60° design log cabin, you can make both diamond and triangle blocks. And you can vary the strips within the blocks. And many beautiful quilts are the result. Page through the pattern section or look at the visual index to find your favorites. This book is organized with general directions for making and assembling the blocks first. You will want to check out this section before you start your chosen quilt. Learn how to cut the shapes you need, and pick up the tips that will make the process more enjoyable such as how to use the charts and diagrams. Then you will find the designs arranged alphabetically. Finally a few borders are at the back of the book. All of these have been included to help you build your own log cabin easily.

Enjoy!

> Throughout the book, Sara has written her favorite method for creating these quilts. Where Marci has a different favorite method, we have given this as an option. Try them to see which one fits you best. In our years of teaching, we have both found that some students are more successful with a different technique, so we hope you find one of these to be your very own frustration-free method.     *—Sara & Marci*

# Basic Beginnings

I made some decisions about how to put these blocks together. For the sake of simplicity, the book is limited to one size of triangle, and one size of diamond. So all the blocks presented in this book are the same size, and interchangeable. Rather than sewing each strip on and then trimming it to the correct size and angle (a technique often used to make log cabin blocks) it turns out to be quicker and more enjoyable to cut the strips to the correct size and shape, and then sew them onto the block.

> Both Sara and I found cutting shapes then sewing to be easiest. However, if your seam allowance is not removing exactly ¼" of fabric, then you may find the technique of trimming after sewing to work best. See the description about seams, pages 26 & 29, for more details. *—Marci*

## FABRIC SELECTION

Though most quilts are best made from blouse weight 100% cotton, log cabin quilts have a tradition of using whatever fabric is available. During the 1930s, being hard up meant your quilt might include all kinds of stuff". Wool, silk, rayon, thin and ravelly cotton were all used. But when they were sewn onto a foundation it made the whole range of fabrics possible. So a couple of the quilts in this book have used silks and/or thin synthetic fabrics, sewing them onto a foundation for stability, like the miniature one shown here. The silks Marci used produce a glowing, iridescent color. Perhaps these fabrics and techniques are best used in wall hangings that will not get the heavy use that a bed quilt is subjected to.

As for the author, the tradition of using whatever fabric is available was a temptation, and I had quite a bit of fun scrounging silks and satins, plus decorator fabrics, at garage sales and in fabric swatch books. I've found that the decorator fabric used to make drapes or to cover a chair is often thicker than the blouse-weight fabric usually used by quilters. This can be OK, depending on what use the quilt will be put to. A wall hanging can be heavier than a soft, cuddly quilt. So with all of my finds, I now have an even larger fabric collection than I had before. Good thing log cabin quilts are a great way to use up scraps.

For value and design, you will find many quilts in this book use "solid" fabrics. There are a few that use larger prints with a variety of color and contrast. Notice the antique quilt shown here. Most fabrics are solid but there are a few plaids, stripes, and 1930s prints that make this quilt shimmer. The value selection between light and dark was successful making the fields and furrows really noticeable. With each quilt, you will find further suggestions and ideas for fabric choices.

### YARDAGE

Since the tradition of log cabin is using scraps, and we encourage a scrappier look, yardages for exact duplication of these quilts is not appropriate. However, a general idea of the amount of fabric needed can help. So, Marci has provided a basic guideline for fabric. She assumed one fabric for all of a particular value. If using a variety of pieces, add an extra ¼ yard for every yard of fabric required. This allows for the extra straightening of the ends. For example, if the amount listed is 1 yd light, and you are using fat quarters, then you need 4 plus 1 fat quarters. For any partial yard, add an extra fat quarter too. So 2¼ yards would be 9 plus 3 fat quarters. Because values may be chosen differently, use the total yardage for the quilt as another basic measure.

The number of shapes which can be cut from 40" strips is listed with the actual size drawings, pages 13-16. Use this and the number of the shape required for the design to determine how many strips of a particular fabric are needed.

*Using a collection of silks from a friend, Marci foundation pieced this design using Clearview Triangle graph paper as the foundation. The lines were easily drawn with the pre-printed grid. Finished size is 12" x 11"*

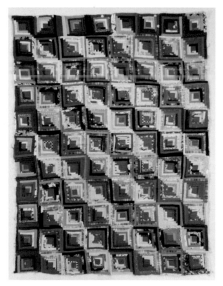

*Maker unknown. This 1930s log cabin was put together from rayon, cotton, silk, wool, nylon, whatever was available, and stabilized by the foundation fabric - great colors!*

## Tools

This book features the 10" Clearview Triangle, a perfect size for these blocks. You may already own the Clearview Triangle 8" ruler or the Super 60. These can also be used, however on the larger logs, and when "truing" the blocks you will need the 10" triangle or a longer straight edge. Caution: If you consider using another manufacturer's 60° ruler, be sure to check your work as other rulers can measure differently than what is illustrated here.

Other required tools are: a rotary cutter, a mat, and a straight ruler like Omnigrid™ for cutting strips.

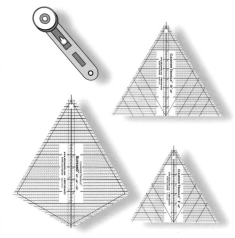

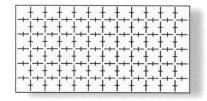

> Use the size of rotary cutter you prefer, although the smallest size is better for cutting around curves (like cutting out clothing patterns), and the two larger sizes save muscle strain, cut faster, and tend to stay on a straight line, more easily.  *—Sara*

## Reading the Patterns

Besides yardages and fabric selection, each pattern has illustrations that show each color-coded block with the number to make and values and sizes of logs. The piecing directions include piecing order, pressing directions, and a color-coded diagram. Use the directions in the next few sections to understand the basics of how to cut shapes and piece the log cabin blocks. For piecing the particular quilt, follow that pattern's step-by-step instructions and diagram.

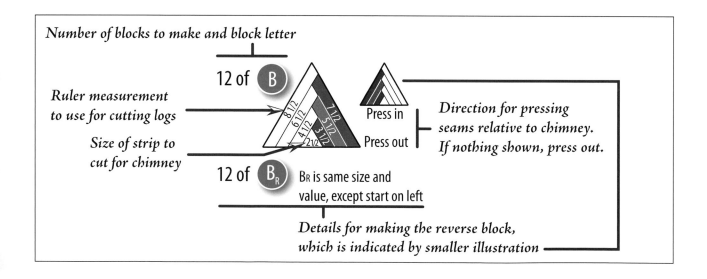

# Cutting Directions – *Index of Shapes*

These cutting methods are based on cutting a strip of fabric then using the 60° ruler to cut a particular shape. Each shape is easy to cut as long as the triangle tool and the strip are kept in mind. By working just with these elements, many shapes can be cut in whatever size is desired. Here is an overview of the shapes used in this book. Use it as a reference once you are familiar with the cuts.

**Triangle**
Page 13

 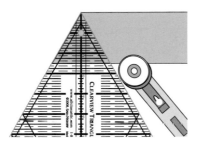

**Diamond**
Page 14

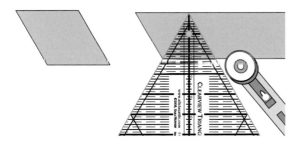

**Triangle Logs**
(a.k.a. flat pyramids)
Page 15

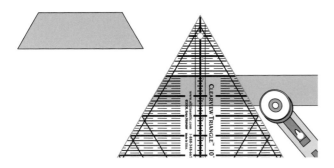

**Diamond Logs**
(a.k.a. long diamonds)
Page 16

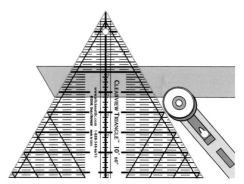

**Triangle Halves**
Page 18

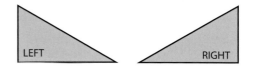

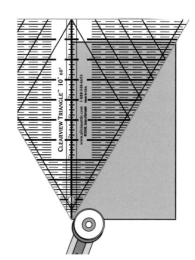

## STRIPS

The first step in cutting any shape is to cut a strip.

1. Fold fabric selvage-to-selvage and press. If pressing from the selvage to the fold produces wrinkles, move the top layer of fabric left or right keeping selvages parallel, until wrinkles disappear.

2. Fold again by bringing the single fold just over the selvage and press.

3. Use a 6" x 12" ruler to measure at the right end of the fabric that the folds are parallel to each other. If they are not parallel, move the single fold up on one side and down on the other until they are parallel. Cut off the ragged or irregular edges of the fabric.

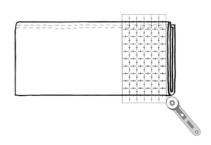

4. Turn the fabric or mat around having the newly trimmed fabric edge on the left. With the ruler aligned cut the strip width required.

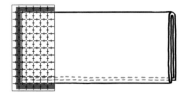

5. If the ruler can not be aligned, turn the fabric back around and make sure folds are parallel. Trim off as needed to straighten the edge.

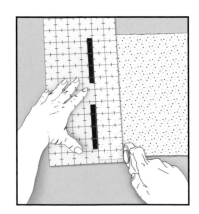

## TRIANGLE

1. Cut a 2½" strip (or a strip the size of the cut triangle).

2. At the right end of the strip, position the ruler with one side along one edge of the strip. Cut the end of the strip to a 60° angle.

3. Rotate the strip so the cut end is to the left. Position the tip of the ruler at corner of the strip and the 2½" line (or the line the size of the triangle) at the edge opposite the corner. Cut along the right side. Check with actual size at right.

4. For the next triangle, rotate the ruler, aligning the point and appropriate rule line, and rotary cut on the right side.

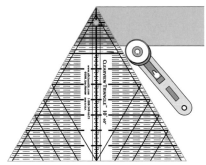

**2½" Triangle Actual Size**
25/40"

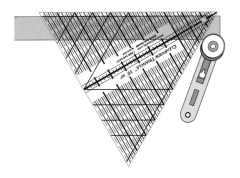

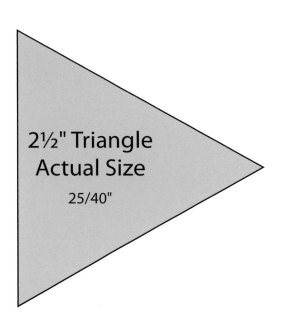

### SPEED CUTTING TRIANGLES

Sara's favorite method requires cutting with both hands or arranging the strip so cutting is controlled. Caution: Do not attempt this if you are not comfortable cutting with both hands or you find yourself cutting towards yourself.

1. Cut a 2½" strip (or a strip the size of the cut triangle).

2. At either end of the strip, position the tip of the ruler at one edge of the strip and the 2½" line (or the line the size of the triangle) at the other edge of the strip.

3. Rotary cut along both sides of the triangle.

Move the tool along the same edge (do not flip it to the other side of the fabric strip) for the next cut. Align the point and appropriate ruler line, and the edge of the ruler with the corner.

4. Cut along both sides of the triangle.

Strips may be stacked up to 6 thicknesses and all cut at once.
    —*Sara*

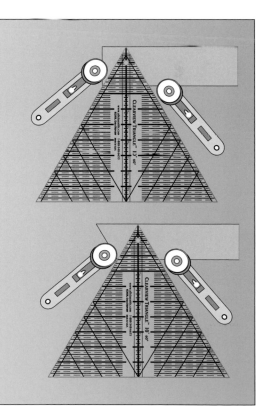

## DIAMOND

1. Cut a 2¼" strip (or a strip the size of the cut diamond) which works with a 2½" triangle.

2. At the right end of the strip, position the ruler with one side along one edge of the strip. Cut the end of the strip to a 60° angle.

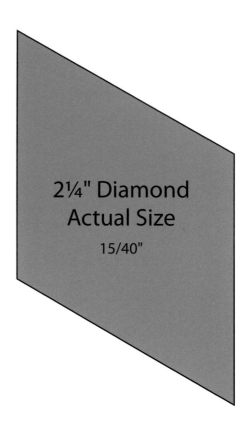

### 2¼" Diamond Actual Size
15/40"

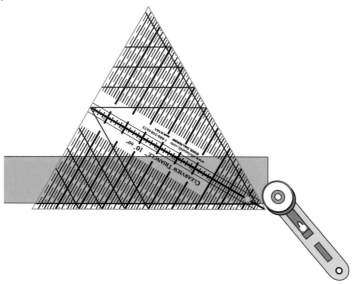

3. Rotate the strip so the cut end is to the left. Place the ruler so the tip is at one edge of the strip, the 2¼" line (or the line the size of the diamond) is along the other edge, and the edge of the ruler is at the corner of the cut end.

4. Rotary cut **only** along the side opposite the first cut. Check with the actual size at right.

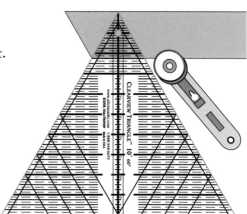

5. Keep moving the tool along the same side of the strip, lining up the cut edge and the side of the tool as shown. Always cut the side opposite the first cut. Strips may be stacked up to 6 thicknesses and all cut at once.

## Triangle Log
(a.k.a. flat pyramid)

1. Cut strip width as required in the pattern. In this book 1½" and 2½" are used most often.

2. At the right end of the strip, position the ruler with one side along one edge of the strip. Cut the end of the strip to a 60° angle.

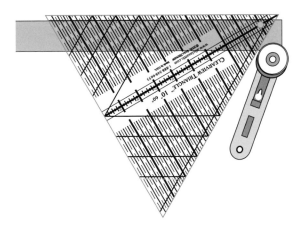

3. Rotate the strip so cut end is to the left. Align the ruler with edge along the cut end, and the size of the log is along the **bottom** edge of the strip. Sizes used here are 3½", 4½"… 8½". The 4½" is illustrated.

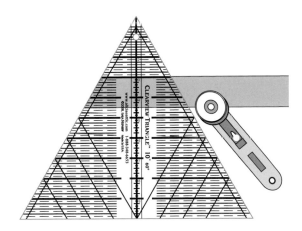

4. Cut along the right side. Check your piece with the actual size at right.

5. Turn the ruler and cut the next triangle log from the other side of the strip with size of the log along **top** edge.

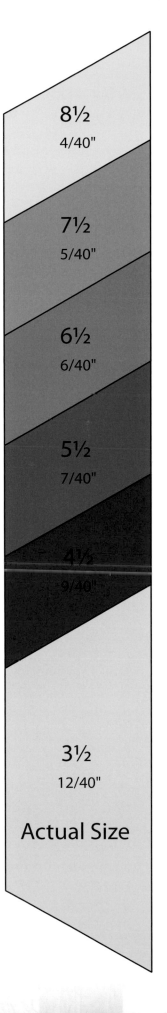

8½
4/40"

7½
5/40"

6½
6/40"

5½
7/40"

4½
9/40"

3½
12/40"

Actual Size

## DIAMOND LOG
(a.k.a. long diamond)

Diamond logs have a reverse of their shape. Check carefully to be sure you are cutting them in the direction required by the pattern. To cut faster, stack the strips all right sides up for a particular size and fabric before cutting. Also, diamond logs may be cut from folded fabric if the design includes a log and its reverse from the same fabric.

**LEFT** (leans to the left)

1. Cut strip width as required in the pattern. In this book, 1½" is used most often.

2. At the right end of the strip, position the ruler with one side along the bottom edge of the strip. Cut the end of the strip to a 60° angle.

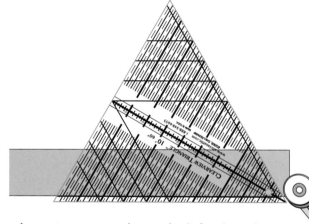

3. Turn the strip so cut end is to the left. Place the ruler point up with edge at the inside corner, and the size of the log is along the bottom edge of the strip. Sizes used here are 2¼", 3¼"… 8¼". The 4¼" is illustrated.

4. Cut along the right side.

Check your piece with the actual size at right.

5. Position ruler the same way for additional diamond logs with size of the log along **top** edge.

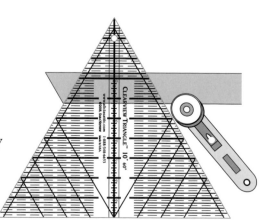

| |
|---|
| 8¼<br>4/40" |
| 7¼<br>4/40" |
| 6¼<br>5/40" |
| 5¼<br>6/40" |
| |
| 3¼<br>10/40" |
| 2¼<br>Left<br>Actual Size<br>16/40" |

**RIGHT** (leans to the right)

1. Cut strip width as required in the pattern. In this book, 1½" is used most often.

2. At the right end of the strip, position the ruler with one side along the top edge of the strip. Cut the end of the strip to a 60° angle.

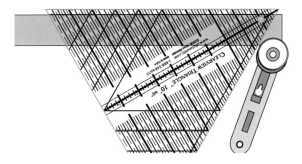

3. Turn the strip so cut end is to the left. Place the ruler point down with edge at the inside corner, and the size of the log is along the top edge of the strip. Sizes used here are 2¼", 3¼"… 8¼". The 4¼" is illustrated.

4. Cut along the right side. Check your piece with the actual size at right.

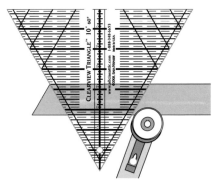

5. Position ruler the same way for additional diamond logs.

Here is another option for cutting these diamond logs, using a rectangular ruler (a right log is illustrated.)

1. After cutting the correct width of strip, trim the end to a 60° angle as in Step 2 above.

2. Use a straight ruler to cut the correct width, parallel to the angled end.  —*Sara*

8¼
4/40"

7¼
4/40"

6¼
5/40"

5¼
6/40"

3¼
10/40"

2¼
**Right
Actual Size**
16/40"

## Triangle Half, Method 1

### Cutting from a Rectangle

To get left and right halves at the same time, lay two rectangles, either right or wrong sides together, cut left or right.

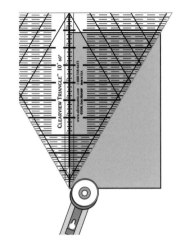

1. Cut a rectangle the height and width needed for the triangle half as given in the directions, for example 5⅛" x 8⅞" which fits the 8½" triangle block.

2 – Left. With the rectangle vertical and the center line of the ruler along the left edge of the rectangle and the tip at the lower left corner, cut the rectangle from corner to corner diagonally.

2 – Right. With the rectangle vertical and the center line of the ruler along the left edge of the rectangle and the tip at the upper left corner, cut the rectangle from corner to corner diagonally.

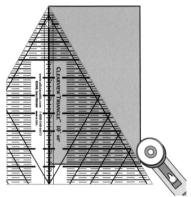

## Triangle Half, Method 2

### Cutting from a Strip

To get left and right at the same time, fold strip in half, cut left or right.

**Left Half**  (L shape when horizontal, points up to left when horizontal)

1. Cut a 2½" strip (or a strip the same size as the cut triangle).

2. At the right end of the strip, square up the end with center line of ruler along the bottom edge and tip to the left. Cut the end to a 90° angle.

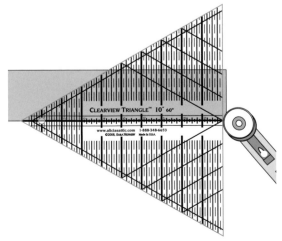

3. Rotate the strip so cut end is to the left. Place tip of the ruler at the bottom of the strip, left-of-center seam line along end of the strip, and 2½" rule line (or the line the size of full triangle) along the top edge of the strip. Cut along right side. Note the tip of the triangle is cut off.

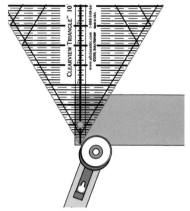

4. Rotate the ruler and place tip of the ruler at the top edge of the strip and left-of-center seam line along the cut end of the strip. Cut along right side.

5. Continue rotating the ruler and arrange as in steps 3 and 4 to cut more shapes. Check the square end of Step 2 on a regular basis and correct as needed.

**Right Half**  (points up to right when horizontal)

1. Cut a 2½" strip (or a strip the same size as the cut triangle).

2. Square the right end of the strip as in Step 2 for Left Half.

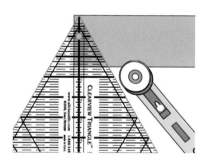

3. Rotate the strip so cut end is to the left. Place tip of the ruler at the bottom of the strip, left-of-center seam line along end of the strip, and 2½" rule line (or the line the size of the full triangle) along the bottom edge of the strip. Cut along right side.

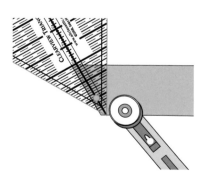

4. Rotate the ruler and place tip of the ruler at the bottom edge of the strip and left-of-center seam line along the cut end of the strip. Cut along right side.

5. Continue rotating the ruler and arrange as in steps 3 and 4 to cut more shapes. Check the square end of Step 2 on a regular basis and correct as needed.

# Triangle Half, Method 3

### Cutting a Large Triangle Half

Some quilt layouts square up the four corners of the design with a very large triangle half which is too large to cut with just the 10" ruler. Using a 24" ruler, 10" 60° ruler, and two pieces of fabric, wrong sides together, that are larger than the measurements of the triangle half, you can cut all four corners at once. This may be a selvage-to-selvage piece of fabric folded selvages together that is at least as long as the longer side of the triangle half. This size will require another long ruler or sliding the long ruler to make the full cut.

What is most important is that you keep the angles correct for it to fit your quilt. So if you would like a piece slightly larger than your quilt, to trim down after sewing, cut any size rectangle that is larger than the triangle half in both directions, and then use the rulers as shown in the diagrams to cut a large triangle half with the correct angles.

1. With the rectangle horizontal, (fold at top if working with folded fabric), place the tip of the 10" ruler at the corner, lining it up at the center perpendicular line (30° angle).

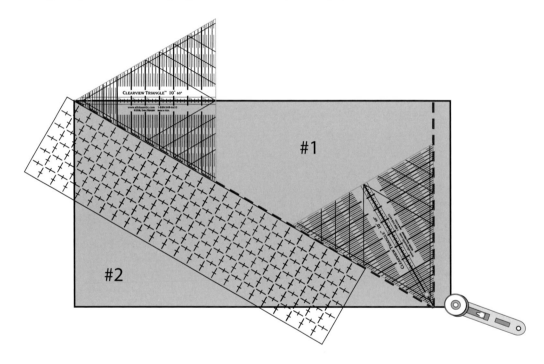

2. Place a long straightedge, like the 24" ruler next to the 10" ruler to extend the cut. Then remove the triangle ruler. Check the other end of the cut with the 10" triangle placed as shown to be sure it is an accurate 60° angle. Rotary cut along the straightedge.

3. Trim off any excess fabric using the 24" ruler to keep it square. (If working with folded fabric, cut along the fold.) This gives two large triangle halves (#1), a right and a left.

4. The other half of the fabric rectangle (#2) gives the other two triangle halves. If needed trim away selvages keeping angles correct.

If a selvage-to-selvage fold is too narrow to cut the large triangle half you need, open the fabric and fold across the complete width, though I have never needed a piece that large.

# Making Triangle and Diamond Blocks

The traditional log cabin block is like a house with a chimney (the center square - usually red) surrounded by logs (concentric strips). In this book, the chimney is either a triangle or a diamond. The logs are added in order by size on all sides or only selected sides creating a wide variety of triangle and diamond blocks. At first I chain-pieced the chimneys and growing blocks onto strips for each log, but quickly I found that I much preferred pre-cutting the diamond and triangle logs and sewing them on individually.

With chain-piecing, I was continually trimming. So the directions given are for pre-cutting the logs and joining the logs to the chimney. If you want to know why chain piecing may work for you, see Marci's hints on pages 26 & 29.

After selecting a quilt pattern from pages 40–109, follow the pattern which has the different blocks shown with how many to make, the values, and sizes of pieces. See examples.

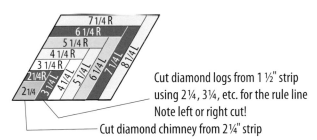

Cut diamond logs from 1 ½" strip using 2 ¼, 3 ¼, etc. for the rule line
Note left or right cut!
Cut diamond chimney from 2 ¼" strip

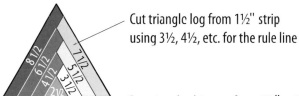

Cut triangle log from 1½" strip using 3½, 4½, etc. for the rule line

Cut triangle chimney from 2½" strip

The chimney, either a triangle or diamond, is cut from a strip the size that is shown in the chimney. Each log is cut from 1½" strips unless the directions state otherwise. The size shown is the measurement line that will align with the fabric, as shown in cutting triangle logs and diamond logs, pages 15 - 17.

Note that triangle logs may be cut from folded fabric, because they are symmetrical. However, diamond logs do have a reverse shape. Check carefully to be sure you are cutting in the direction required by the pattern, either left or right. **The 'L' and 'R' refer to the "lean" of the log, not the position in the block.** Because the size of these logs is so important, we have included actual sizes for checking.

> Another measurement that is important is using a scant ¼" seam. Check the seams occasionally until you are confident of accuracy. In general press each log out from the chimney before adding another. Press across the strip, not along the strip. Too much pressing can distort the growing block. Marci has suggested some pressing which is in toward the chimney so that seams are pre-pressed to lock. I twist seams as needed as I sew. Choose which way works best for you.      —*Sara*

Why sew with a scant quarter inch seam? When designs are made, the designer is assuming that when you are done cutting, sewing, and pressing, you have only removed ¼" from the front of the fabrics. So when you are measuring exactly ¼" on the back, the roll of the fabric around the thread can take away from the front of the design. Therefore, you will want to measure and sew with a scant ¼" on the back, giving you a design that fits what was intended. To test your seam, sew three 2"x10" strips together. Press the seams one direction and measure the strip set. It should be 5" across.     —*Marci*

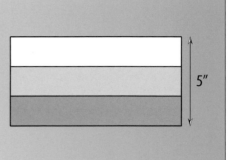

Consider using Qtools Sewing Edge to make your sewing easier and consistent with a scant ¼". Replacing the masking tape or moleskin you may be using on the bed of your machine, Sewing Edge creates a stop without leaving a sticky mess or having to layer it. You can reposition it and use it over and over. The thickness is a little more than two layers of cotton fabric so it works even with flannel and is thin enough so any "ears" go right over the strip. Use it even with your ¼" foot because you can guide and align your fabric before the foot and needle and stop and make adjustments rather than when it is too late at the foot. When I use Sewing Edge, I can sew even faster and keep the seam consistent. Even I am amazed at the neatness of my work, especially with my limited sewing time.     —*Marci*

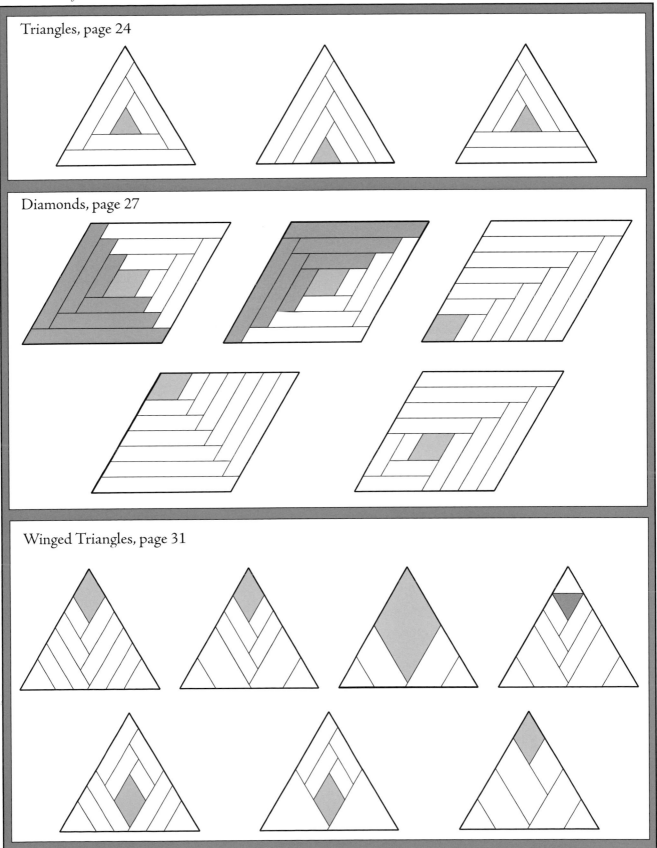

Triangles, page 24

Diamonds, page 27

Winged Triangles, page 31

Use copies of this page for value & color placement to create your own designs.

## TRIANGLE BLOCKS

Make copies of this table and use them to plan placement and for ease in cutting.

| Pattern: | | Block: |
|---|---|---|
| # (per 40") | L, M, or D | Size |
| 1 (12) | | 3 ½ |
| 2 (9) | | 4 ½ |
| 3 (7) | | 5 ½ |
| 4 (6) | | 6 ½ |
| 5 (5) | | 7 ½ |
| 6 (4) | | 8 ½ |

1. Add the first triangle log to the chimney and press out from the center.

2. Add the triangle logs in order by size being consistent whether you turn the block clockwise (CW) or counterclockwise (CCW) to seam on the next piece.

3. The triangle block should measure 8 ½" when complete. Trim only if/as necessary, by lining up the center lines of the ruler along points. On the triangle with the chimney at the base, trim the base side first.

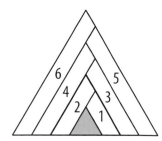
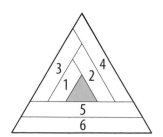
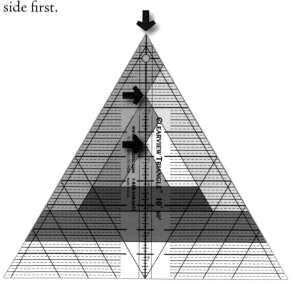

If using repetitive fabrics, you may wish to strip-piece the triangle chimney with the first log.

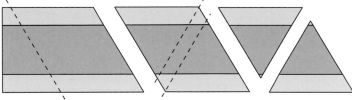

Here's how:

1. Cut one 2¼" strip of chimney fabric and two 1½" strips of first log fabric.

2. Sew strips together lengthwise with chimney fabric in the middle. Press seams out. Trim a 60° angle at right end.

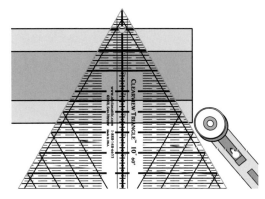

3. Turn fabric, and cut 3½" wide slices from this set of strips. Keep seam aligned.

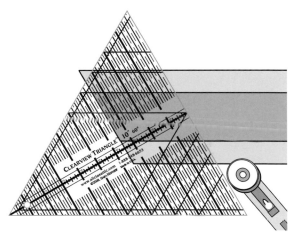

4. From each slice, cut two 3½" triangles - line up 3½" rule line to outside edge of the strip. You will need to turn the slice to get the second triangle.

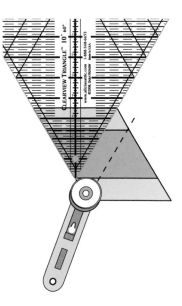

Press each log out from the center, before adding another, using a hot, dry iron. Press across the strip, not along the strip. Too much pressing can distort the growing triangle. —*Sara*

To check that you are staying true to the finished size, you can measure the block after adding any log. It should be the size of the log just added. For example, after adding the 5½" log, the triangle should measure 5½". *—Marci*

When adding a log to a triangle, the seam has two ears from the triangle sticking out. Make them equal in size.

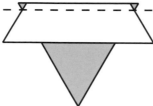

Ideally the base of the ear will match your seam allowance. Sometimes because of variances in cutting and piecing, they aren't quite the right size. If the ears are consistently too small, or your triangle has edges of the new log sticking out on both sides, your seam allowance is bigger than the design is expecting.

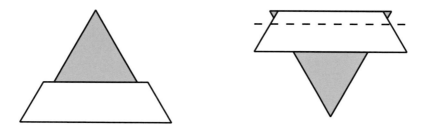

Try piecing the triangles onto a strip, pressing seam toward the strip, and trimming to fit your seam allowance.

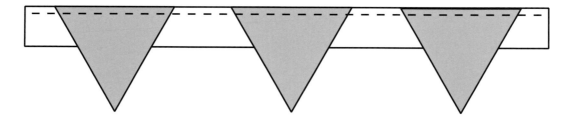

Your blocks will be smaller, but as long as you are consistent, they should come together in the end. Between triangles leave enough space, about the width of the strip, to cut the correct angles.

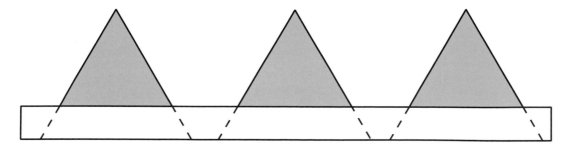

## DIAMOND BLOCKS

1. Sew on the first diamond log to the appropriate side of the diamond chimney and press out from the center, unless suggested otherwise.

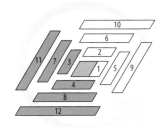

2. Sew on the diamond logs in order by size. Be consistent whether you turn clockwise or counterclockwise to seam on the next piece. Note that the chimney is sometimes in the center, off to one end or side, and even off center. You always start with the chimney and add logs so it ends up in the particular position.

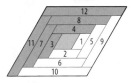

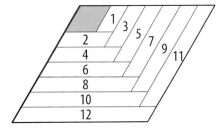
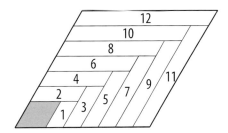
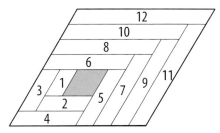

3. The diamond block should measure 8¼" when finished with 60° angles at the ends and 120° on the sides. Use the ruler aligning center points and cross points as shown to measure. Notice how diagonal ruler lines align with seams. Trim only as necessary. Make it an exact 8¼" diamond.

If using repetitive fabrics, you may wish to strip-piece the diamond chimney with the first log.

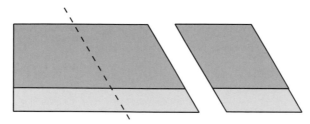

Here's how:

1. Cut a 2¼" strip of the chimney fabric and a 1½" strip of the first strip fabric.
2. Sew together lengthwise and press seam toward first log strip. Trim the end of this set of strips to the needed 60° angle.

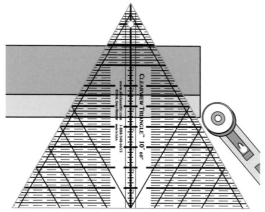

3. Then cut 2¼" sections from this set of strips, checking your angle.

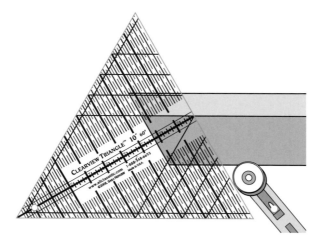

To check that you are staying true to the finished size, you can measure the block after adding any log. If an odd number of logs have been added, the measurement will be the log size one direction and an inch more the other direction. For example, after adding the second 4¼" (the 5th log) the diamond will measure 4¼" one direction and 5¼" the other. If an even number of logs have been added, the measurement will be the log size both directions. Add the 6th log, (the first 5¼") and the diamond will measure 5¼" both directions.  —*Marci*

When adding a log to a diamond, the seam has two ears sticking out, one from the diamond and one from the log.

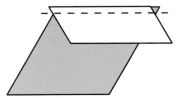

The size is changed by sliding one to the right or to the left of the other with the edges still aligned. Make the ears match your seam allowance.

Sometimes because of variances in cutting and piecing, one may be too large or too small and the other perfect. In this case, make one of them slightly smaller and the other slightly larger than they should be. This splits any variances in half and puts it in the seam allowance. After sewing if your pieces are staggered, then the ears are not matching your seam allowance and need to be adjusted.

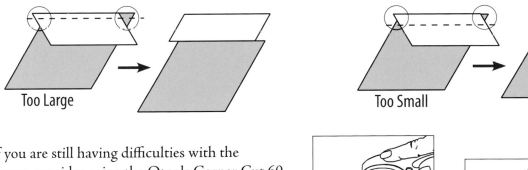

If you are still having difficulties with the seams, consider using the Qtools Corner Cut 60 to trim the ears prior to sewing.

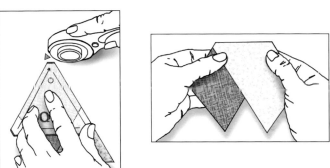

Another option would be to sew the diamonds onto a strip, press toward strip, unless indicated otherwise, and trim to fit.

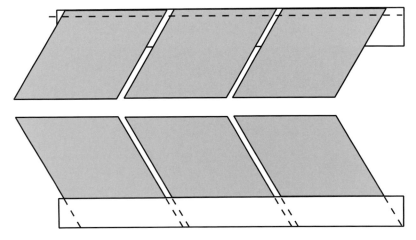

As long as you are consistent with the size of seam allowance, the blocks should come together.

| Pattern: | | Block: | |
|---|---|---|---|
| **# (per 40 )** | **L, M, or D** | **Size** | L or R |
| 1 (16) | | 2 ¼ | |
| 2 (10) | | 3 ¼ | |
| 3 (10) | | 3 ¼ | |
| 4 (8) | | 4 ¼ | |
| 5 (8) | | 4 ¼ | |
| 6 (6) | | 5 ¼ | |
| 7 (6) | | 5 ¼ | |
| 8 (5) | | 6 ¼ | |
| 9 (5) | | 6 ¼ | |
| 10 (4) | | 7 ¼ | |
| 11 (4) | | 7 ¼ | |
| 12 (4) | | 8 ¼ | |

It was a hot summer's day and my granddaughter Ashley was wanting to chat while I worked. I produced an unprecedented number of long diamonds cut in the *wrong* direction, to the *wrong* size, or from the *wrong* fabric. So I've created a chart to simplify the cutting (see above). Copy this chart on a copy machine or simply draw it for yourself on a piece of paper. This will help you choose the correct fabric and cut the angle of the long diamond in the correct direction.

I like to print or copy my charts and pattern pages onto card stock. This makes stiff pages you can lean against a wall or a window for easy seeing while you cut shapes or sew. Another way to get the same result is to put regular paper pages into a plastic holder they sell at office supply stores. It's like a page protector, but heavier, and it has a hole at the top for hanging on a wall.

To use the chart, write the name of the pattern you are making at the top of the page. If it has more than one kind of diamond in the pattern, mark with the letter in the box at upper right. Transfer the information about value and right or left to the chart from the diagram in the pattern. —*Sara*

## WINGED TRIANGLE BLOCKS

These blocks are a combination of a diamond center and two triangles on the sides, which are the wings of the finished triangle block. Refer to basic triangle and diamond instructions if needed.

1. Sew on the first diamond log to one side of the diamond chimney and press out from the center, unless indicated otherwise. For faster method see strip-piecing for diamond chimneys, page 28.

2. Sew on the diamond logs in order by size to make a 4¼" diamond. Be consistent whether you turn clockwise or counterclockwise to seam on the next log.

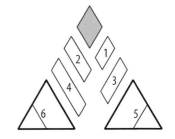

3. Make two 4¾" triangles, called wings, using triangle logs as listed in the directions for the pattern or speed up your piecing by strip piecing the wings as described on page 32.

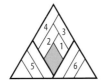    

4. Sew the wings onto the 4¼" diamond, always from the left or right edge down. Never sew from the bottom edge up. The first wing sewn on has an extra ¼" at the bottom. The second wing overlaps the first and this point will be about ½" from the edge. It is not meant to be at the seam allowance line.

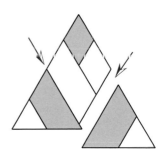

5. The triangle block should measure 8½" when complete. Trim only if/as necessary, by lining up the center lines of the ruler along points. Trim the left and right edges first.

When adding the wings to the diamond, the seam has one ear from the triangle at the wider angle on the diamond, and the edge of the triangle is out past the narrower angle on the diamond.

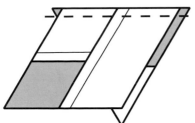

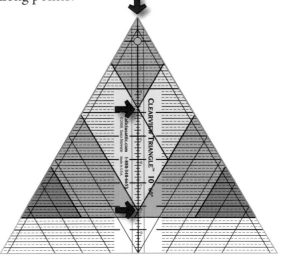

# Variations and Strip-Piecing Wings
## Sandwich-Pieced Diamond Chimney
(Used in Flower Petal and Star Sampler)

1. Cut 2½" strips from two different fabrics which are usually one light and one dark. Seam these strips right sides together with a ¼" seam down both sides.

2. Cut triangles from this set of strips.

3. Pull the tips of the seamed triangles apart and press toward the dark.

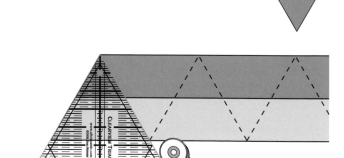

## Two Strip Wings:
### Method 1:

1. Cut a light and a dark 2⅝" strip and sew together lengthwise. Press to the dark.

2. Cut 4¾" triangles from this set of strips. You will get dark-based and light-based triangles. Choose which (dark- or light-based) you wish to use, and set the others aside for another quilt.

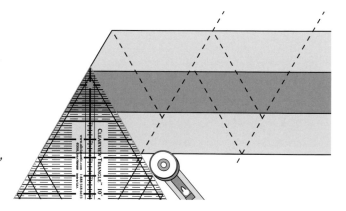

### Method 2:

1. Cut two 2⅝" base strips and one 2⅝" tip strip. Sew together lengthwise with tip strip in the middle. Press away from center.

2. Cut 4¾" slices from this set of strips. Then cut two - 4¾" triangles from each slice. See strip-pieced triangle chimneys, page 25. There will be some waste, but more speed.

## Three Strip Wings:

1. Cut two 1½" strips for triangle logs and one 3" strip for triangle tip. Sew strips together lengthwise with tip strip in the middle, then smaller log strip on both sides, then finally the base log strip on both sides. Press seams from center out.

2. Cut 4¾" slices from this set of strips. Then cut two - 4¾" triangles from each slice. See strip-pieced triangle chimney, page 25. There will be some waste, but more speed than cutting pieces individually.

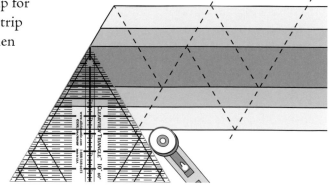

## OLD-FASHIONED FOUNDATION PIECING

One of the fun things about old log cabin quilts is looking to see all the different fabrics the quilters used in their blocks. Because the traditional log cabin block was foundation pieced, they could use a wide variety of material. And we can do the same today.

Just cut a triangle or a diamond at the proper size (in this book, an 8½" triangle or an 8¼" diamond) from a quilting fabric you no longer want to put on the front of a quilt, fabric from a garage sale, or any light-weight cotton fabric. If the chimney will be in the center of the block, draw lines from corner to corner on a diamond or down the three centers on a triangle.

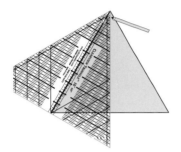 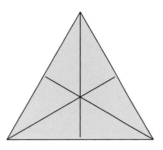 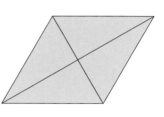

Then use the lines to center the chimney precisely. Put each point of the shape on the lines drawn.

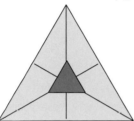 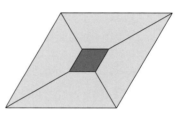

Place the first log on the chimney as you would if there was no foundation fabric and sew the scant ¼" seam through all three layers.

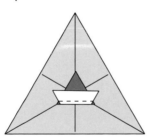 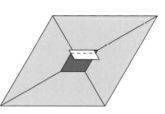

Keep sewing the logs onto the growing block. I found that the foundation tended to shrink slightly, so for the final two strips of the triangle, I cut the strip at 1¾" and cut it at the line on the ruler up to ¼" bigger than the chart calls for. Then I trimmed the triangle to exactly 8½". You could make a similar adjustment to the diamonds if necessary.

I don't necessarily recommend foundation piecing, but if you have wanted to play with old ties, or scraps of silk, brocade, rayon - any flashy and hard to deal with fabrics, the use of foundation fabric will help tame these beautiful but wild creatures.          —*Sara*

# Joining Blocks and Setting Pieces

In this section, we differ on our preferred methods. Layout your blocks and follow the specific pattern directions for joining them. Pick your favorite piecing and pressing techniques from the following and have fun building your log cabin quilt.

### Joining Blocks, From Sara:

I twist seams as needed to allow seam intersections to butt up against each other, making points come together well and reducing bulk. One exception is where three pieces come together at one point, to make a half-hexagon, I recommend pressing away from this point in both directions.

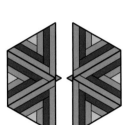

(To use this method for any half-hexagons, replace pressing instructions in the patterns with pressing both out.) This creates little 60° points that stick out past the fabric edge. Do not trim these off. They are useful to help align the units for accurate sewing. Trim them after the block or top is pieced if they will show through a light fabric.

When six fabrics meet at one point, pinch the center where the seams cross, open the fabric to see how the seams are meeting and adjust as necessary. Pin to hold while stitching.

The mild bias of the 60° triangle aids in lining up seams. Pull a little if necessary. All seams are pressed to one side to make the quilt top durable. When blocks are finished, press from the top with a wet press cloth.

### Joining Blocks, From Marci:

With each block I have indicated the direction to press seams so when they are joined into the quilt top, the seams oppose each other or butt up against each other. In the diagrams, the small triangles on the dashed seam lines and at the ends of some rows indicate the direction to press the seam. Note that some are twisted so that one end is up, the other end down. Figuring this out ahead of time is definitely part of the engineer in me.

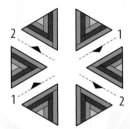

Where three pieces come together at one point, to make a half-hexagon, I recommend sewing them together always in a clockwise order and pressing seams clockwise. This creates seams that oppose each other throughout the quilt. If you like seams that butt against each other, then anytime half-hexagons are made in the design, piece and press clockwise, and then join them with other pieces as indicated.

When I first started working with 60° designs in 1987, I worried about having seams on the bias edges. Over the years I have come to realize that the bias of this angle makes the project come together more easily than straight grain would offer. Also, it is not as stretchy as true bias and therefore is easier to work with.

I use steam when pressing, but I also recommend it only to those who are comfortable with it. If you find fabric stretching when pressing, then work with a dry iron and follow Sara's suggestions of using a pressing cloth at the end.

# MEASURING FOR SETTING TRIANGLES

To square up each quilt, triangle halves are cut from rectangles. These final pieces need to fit the piecing that you have done throughout the quilt. Measure your triangles and diamonds as follows. Use the table on the next page to determine the best fit. These numbers account for seam allowances.

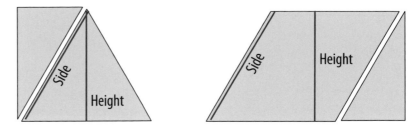

## Triangles

1. Measure the side of several triangles. Using the average measurement, divide by 2 and add ¼" for the width of the rectangle.

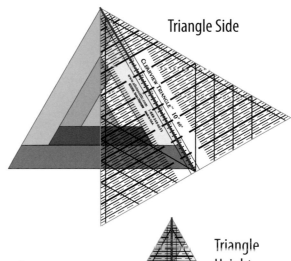

Triangle Side

2. Measure the height of several triangles, from tip to base, as shown. Using the average measurement, add ⅜" for the length of the rectangle.

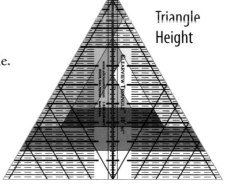

Triangle Height

## Diamonds

1. Measure the sides of the diamonds. Divide the average measurement by two, and then add ⅜" for the width of the rectangle.

Diamond Side

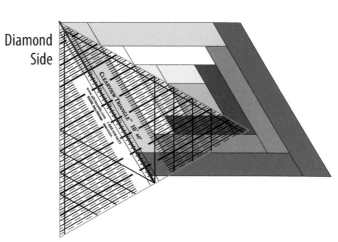

2. With two sides of the diamond horizontal, measure the height of the diamond from one edge to the opposite edge using a long ruler. Have the lines of the ruler aligned perpendicular with the edge of the diamond as shown. Using the average measurement, add ⅝" for the length of the rectangle.

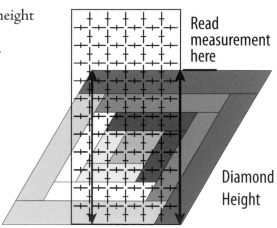

Read measurement here

Diamond Height

Use the table to check some common measurements. Your numbers should match a particular pair. If not an exact match, use a size larger and trim down later. Once you have the size, cut the rectangles and follow instructions for cutting triangle halves on page 18.

| Triangle | | Diamond | | Rectangle to cut | |
|---|---|---|---|---|---|
| **Side** | **Height** | **Side** | **Height** | **Width** | **Length** |
| 9 ½" | 8 ¼" | 9 ¼" | 8" | 5" | 8 $^5/_8$" |
| 9 $^7/_8$" | 8 ½" | 9 ½" | 8 ¼" | 5 $^1/_8$" | 8 $^7/_8$" |
| 10 $^1/_8$" | 8 ¾" | 9 $^7/_8$" | 8 ½" | 5 ¼" | 9 $^1/_8$" |
| 18 ½" | 16" | 18 $^1/_8$" | 15 ¾" | 9 ½" | 16 $^3/_8$" |
| 18 ¾" | 16 ¼" | 18 ½" | 16" | 9 $^5/_8$" | 16 $^5/_8$" |
| 19" | 16 ½" | 18 ¾" | 16 ¼" | 9 ¾" | 16 $^7/_8$" |

## SETTING STARS FOR DOGWOOD STAR AND MONTANA

A gorgeous quilt with a difference! Linda DeGaeta helped the author work out the correct math for the Dogwood Star, testing the pattern multiple times. This version, called Sarabande, used a strip of fabric to fit the floating stars to the star diamonds.

So that you won't have to determine a strip size to float your stars like Linda did in Sarabande, measure your star diamond as described in the previous section. If you use 3⅜" wing triangles, 3⅛" diamonds, and 6" corner triangles, the setting triangle comes out ¼" larger than needed at 16½". Sew the triangles onto the diamond working from the outside corners to the narrow point, as done for winged triangle blocks page 31. The excess ¼" will overlap and allow the points of the diamond to float – an easy solution.

Because of the large size of the diamond involved and the variances of seam allowance that can occur, here is a chart to use to select the best size that will fit your diamonds. From the chart, cut the small diamond, small wing triangle, and large corner triangles. These numbers will replace the ones listed for your pattern, which are the shaded row.

**Sarabande 56" x 64"**
*Linda's choice of color and playfulness with quilt designs produces gorgeous quilts. The creamy blue and soft pastels in these fabrics contrasts with the stronger dark blues and the black, producing a moonlit radiance, and is a color scheme she has used before. Machine pieced by Linda DeGaeta, machine quilted by Janice Jamison.*

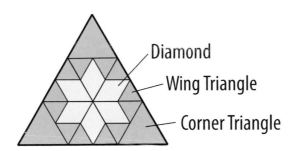

Diamond
Wing Triangle
Corner Triangle

| Average Star Diamond | Setting Triangle Size to Make | Diamond Cut Size | Wing Triangle Cut Size | Corner Triangle Cut Size |
|---|---|---|---|---|
| Up to 15 ½" | 15 ¾" | 3" | 3 ¼" | 5 ¾" |
| 15 ¾" – 16 ¼" | 16 ½" | 3 ⅛" | 3 ⅜" | 6" |
| 16 ½" – 17" | 17 ¼" | 3 ¼" | 3 ½" | 6 ¼" |

# Binding for Other Angles

Several of these quilts finish out to a hexagonal shape. Here is how to miter the corners for angles other than 90 degrees. (Uses ¼" seam allowance.)

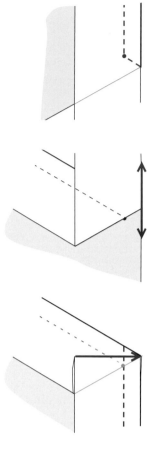

1. At the corner, stop at the point where seam lines cross, ¼" away from the edges, with needle down in fabric. Pivot toward corner point and sew off edge of quilt.

2. Remove quilt from machine and turn it to work on the next side. Fold the binding back along angled seam line. Align the binding edges with edge of next side of quilt top, making a straight line.

3. Fold binding down, in line with the corner of the top, keep binding edge and quilt top edge aligned. This works for angles wider and narrower than a square corner. On narrower angles, you may need to trim back some of the fabric folded inside.

4. On the back side, fold right side in, then left side. Again you may need to trim fabric on the narrower angles.

# Create your Own Designs

There are so many possible variations of a log cabin diamond or triangle that this book has barely scratched the surface. Try something different with your design like Linda DeGaeta did in Badge of Honor. She substituted a wider strip with a narrow strip of green for several of the other logs.

You can substitute a 2½" strip for two 1½" strips, especially if you have lots of layers of strips to make and want something faster. Or, split the 1½" strip into two 1" strips for an extra added feature as Sara did with the black and white strips in Beauty of Africa. This created an interwoven effect, which is why this quilt is one of Marci's favorites.

Also consider making the position of the logs different than the original design. Changing *where* you add the strip will change the design of the quilt, sometimes a lot and sometimes only a little. Play with the fabric selections, the placement of value, or changing the size of the pieces. Perhaps adding a strip is the same as painting with a brushstroke. Working with color and value brings out the beauty of these patterns, and makes them fun.

Here are examples of changing the strips for the design Stripped Stars.

In the first variation, we pieced the same blocks and rotated the triangles in the layout so that the longest log was on the outside. This created a ring around each hexagon and makes the star have a twist or spinning affect.

The second variation was shifting the values on the pieced triangle so it ended with the longest log and single value on the outside. Again, the ring is around each hexagon, but the stars have a more symmetrical look. This is similar to Winter Snow.

Each design is different with a single change. Try your hand at a planned difference or use a mistake as an opportunity to create your very own log cabin design. You will be surprised at how a simple change can make the quilt simply amazing!

We hope you have enjoyed building *your* log cabin quilt. It is definitely not your grandmother's! Share your creations with us and others by submitting them to our website, www.aliciasattic.com. There you will find more options for these quilts with even more designs…the book had to be limited but our imaginations are not! Enjoy your quilting!

Sara and Marci

Original

Rotated Triangle

Values Shifted

**3D Logs**
by Sara Nephew • Page 42

**Alexander's Star**
by Janice Jamison • Page 44

**Badge of Honor**
by Linda DeGaeta • Page 46

**Beauty of Africa**
by Sara Nephew • Page 48

**Birth of Stars**
by Kathy Springer • Page 50

**Chinoiserie**
by Linda DeGaeta • Page 52

**Chrysanthemum**
by Sara Nephew • Page 56

**Dawn Star**
by Marci Baker • Page 60

**Dogwood Star**
by Linda DeGaeta • Page 62

**Eagles Wings**
by Sara Nephew • Page 64

**Fireworks**
by Scott Hansen • Page 66

**Flags Flying**
by Sara Nephew • Page 68

**Flower Petal**
by Linda Tellesbo • Page 70

**Frost**
by Janet Goad • Page 72

**Frost Star**
by Linda DeGaeta • Page 74

**Frosty Windows**
by Bobbie Crosby • Page 76

**Glory**
by Diane Coombs ✦ Page 78

**Iris**
by Diane Coombs ✦ Page 80

**Mexican Star**
by Sara Nephew ✦ Page 82

**Montana**
by Kathie Kryla ✦ Page 84

**Native Blanket**
by Bonnie Walker ✦ Page 86

**Ornament**
by Kathy Syring ✦ Page 88

**Owls**
by Joan Dawson ✦ Page 90

**Painted Desert**
by Kathy Syring ✦ Page 92

**Shield**
by Janice Jamison ✦ Page 94

**Star Sampler**
by Joyce Cambron ✦ Page 96

**Stripped Star**
by Linda DeGaeta ✦ Page 98

**Tropical**
by Sarah Newman ✦ Page 100

**Tulip**
by Linda DeGaeta ✦ Page 102

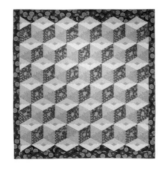

**Tumbling Logs**
by Terri Shinn ✦ Page 104

**Will-O-Wisp**
by Kathy Syring ✦ Page 106

**Winter Snow**
by Sara Nephew ✦ Page 108

*Spanish Dance*
**51" x 60"**
pieced by Sara Nephew,
machine quilted by Judy Irish

# 3-D Logs

## 47" x 58"

| Fabrics: | Yards: |
|---|---|
| Chimneys | 3/8 |
| Light | 1 |
| Medium | 1 3/4 |
| Dark | 1 1/2 |

One simple triangle block – arranged for a variety of 3-D designs – your choice! Sara played with the triangle blocks by piecing some with logs in clockwise order, and some counterclockwise, creating a different angle for the white spaceships along the sides. Soft dappled batiks from the Fabric Freedom Collection enhance the play of light and dark over the surface of the quilt.

- See general directions, pgs. 8-32, for cutting, piecing, and pressing.
- Make quantity of blocks listed using 1½" wide strips for logs.
- Sew triangle blocks into rows beginning at opposite ends and pressing away from that end. This will allow all of the seams to lock together.
- Add borders as desired.
- Consider other sizes. Here are a few options:

| Triangles (across x down) | 4 x 7 | 7 x 14 | 9 x 18 |
|---|---|---|---|
| Finished Size | 31 x 36 | 54 x 67 | 70 x 85 |

72 of

Press out, except last seam in

Cut 6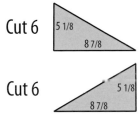

Cut 6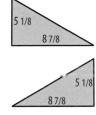

3-D Logs Optional Layout:

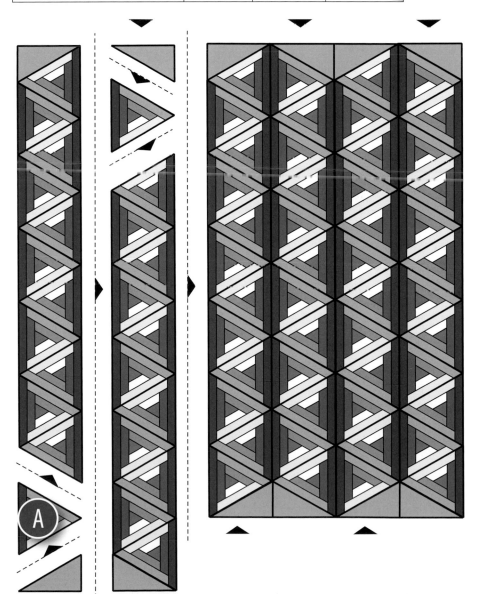

*Alexander's Star*

**60" x 70"**

Pieced & Machine Quilted

by Janice Jamison

# Alexander's Star

54" x 62"

This quilt is an excellent example of the impact of simplicity. Janice chose blending yellows to emphasize the double-pointed inner star, and then added the six blue star tips. Concentrating on just two colors seems simple, but results in a surprising complexity of design. She did some fussy-cutting too, as seen in the floral design repeating in each blue point. Crystals on the dark background create sparkling dots for added interest. Beautiful tight quilted feather patterns fill the surface of the star.

+ See general directions, pgs. 8-32, for cutting, piecing, and pressing.
+ Make quantity of blocks listed using 1½" wide strips for logs.
+ In each wedge, sew C to B then to A, and D to C. Sew these units together with triangle halves to make 6 wedges. Note the twisted seam between B and A.
+ Sew the wedges into groups of 3 and sew across the middle to complete the center hexagon. Add corner triangle halves. Add borders as desired.

| Fabrics: | Yards: |
|---|---|
| Light | 1 |
| Medium | 1 1/4 |
| Dark | 3/4 |
| Background | 2 1/4 |

6 of **A**

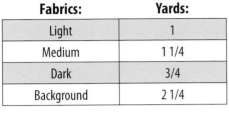

Press in

6 of **B**

Press out

12 of **C**

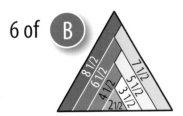

Press 6 in, 6 out

6 of **D**

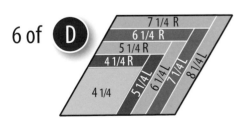

Press out

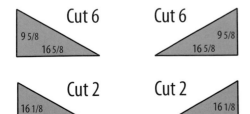

Cut 6    Cut 6

Cut 2    Cut 2

*Tropical Mandala*

**78" x 86"**

Pieced by Linda DeGaeta

Machine Quilted by Janice Jamison

**62" x 72"**

Linda interpreted this pattern like a travelogue to an exotic destination. The fabric, though it may have a floral look, actually is mostly about fish. Tropical flowers and tropical fish! How about a trip to Hawaii or Tahiti? Maybe someday. In the meantime, just relax and study this beautiful presentation like the fine line in light green and another in light blue just inside the pieced border.

- See general directions, pgs. 8-32, for cutting, piecing, and pressing.
- Make quantity of blocks listed using 1½" wide strips for logs.
- To duplicate fine green line around the quilt center, use the Alternate B block and its reverse.
- Choose to make the two rows of Block D, inner (18 blocks) and outer (16 blocks) either the same or different.
- Piece 6 wedges, 2 side border units and 4 corner units as shown.
- Alternating direction of pressing for A, layout units. Add side border units to side wedges. Sew the wedges into groups of 3. Add corner units and sew through middle. Add borders as desired.

| Fabrics: | Yards: |
|---|---|
| Light | 2 3/4 |
| Medium | 2 |
| Dark | 2 1/2 |

**6 of** (A)
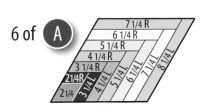
Press 3 in, 3 out

**6 of** (B)
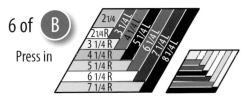
Press in

**6 of** (B_R)
B_R is same size and value, cut opposite direction
Press out

**12 of** (C)

**16 + 18 of** (D)
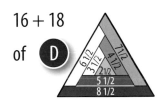

**18 of** (E)

**4 of** (F)
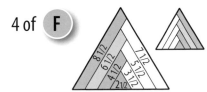

**4 of** (F_R)
F_R is same size and value, start on left

**Cut 8**
5 1/8
8 7/8

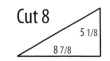
**Cut 8**
5 1/8
8 7/8

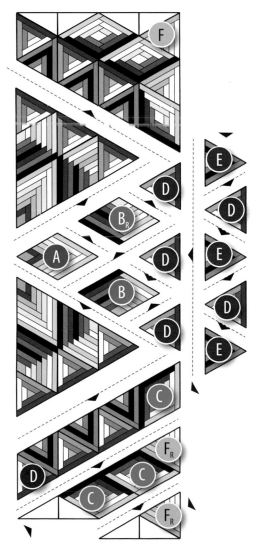

**Alternate** (B)

Beauty of Africa

**79" x 89"**

Pieced by Sara Nephew

Machine Quilted by

Yvette Ebaugh

# Beauty of Africa

77" x 90"

This quilt was made from the author's collection of African fabrics and related textiles, obtained at church sales, garage sales, and on eBay. The fabrics are mainly wax-resist batiks in strong colors and large prints, but cutting them into narrow strips changes everything. A couple of plain colors are added, black and white, creating the interwoven design and the scattered bright stars. And woven ikat shawls from Java make perfect borders on the sides.

- See general directions, pgs. 8-32, for cutting, piecing, and pressing, especially for winged triangles, B, page 31.
- Make quantity of blocks listed using 1½" wide strips for A logs and 2½" for B logs.
- Make 36 wedges, each wedge has 1 A and 2 B's.
- Alternating direction of pressing for A, make 12 half-blocks from 3 wedges each. Choose pressing, pg. 34. Sew into rows as shown. Add an 8" border to both sides.

| Fabrics: | Yards: |
|---|---|
| Light | 1 1/4 |
| Medium | 4 1/2 |
| Dark | 3 3/4 |
| Border | 3 |

36 of

Press left logs in,
right logs out

72 of

Press left logs in,
right logs out

Cut 4     Cut 4

9 5/8     9 5/8
16 5/8    16 5/8

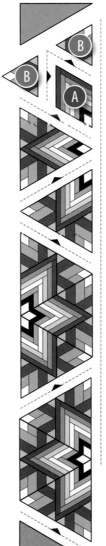

*Birth of Stars*

**78" x 86"**

Pieced by Kathleen Springer

Quilted by Marianne Roan

# Birth of Stars

62" x 72"

| Fabrics: | Yards: |
|---|---|
| Very Light | 2 |
| Light | 2 1/4 |
| Medium | 1 3/4 |
| Dark | 1 1/2 |
| Very Dark | 1 1/8 |

This is a quick quilt with lots of impact. Kathleen chose colors that definitely evoke a night sky saturated with stars… maybe even falling stars. And the border adds the mystery of distant galaxies. Is this a "go-to-sleep in the night" quilt or what? Yet it would be wonderful as a wall hanging too.

- See general directions, pgs. 8-32, for cutting, piecing, and pressing.
- Make quantity of blocks listed using 1½" wide strips for logs.
- Note that the winged triangles have a slight overlap at the bottom, center point. Also this point should not match when blocks are sewn together.
- Make 20 half-blocks, with 3 A's each. Make 20 half-blocks, with 3 B's each. Choose pressing, pg. 34.
- Sew into rows as shown. Add borders as desired.

60 of

Press left logs in,
right logs out

60 of

Press left logs in,
right logs out

 Cut 8     Cut 8

*Dragon's Claw*
**62" x 77"**
Pieced by Linda DeGaeta
Machine Quilted by Janice Jamison

# Chinoiserie

**62" x 72"**

| Fabrics: | Yards: |
|---|---|
| Light | 3 |
| Medium | 1 3/4 |
| Dark | 2 |

Asian derived patterns on the fabric with dragons, brush lettering, chrysanthemums, and the like creates a striking, high contrast quilt in red, black, and tan colors. The motif goes well with the jagged lines and sharp edges of the overlapping log strips. The unusual quilting pattern seems to add a flavor of antiquity to the rich details.

- See general directions, pgs. 8-32, for cutting, piecing, and pressing.
- Make quantity of blocks listed using 1½" wide strips for logs, except use 2½" wide for wings of C, and 2⅜" for 3⅝" triangle log of F.
- Note that C has an overlap at the bottom, center point where F does not.
- For D, after adding 4¾" log, trim triangle to 4½" then add 4 remaining logs.
- Make 6 wedges from 1 A, 3 B's, 3 Br's, 1 C, 1 Cr, 1 D, 1 E, 1 Er, and 1 F.
- Make corner units from 1 C, 1 Cr, and 2 G's and setting triangles.
- Sew wedges three and three and sew across middle. Add corner units. Add borders as desired.

6 of **A**

Press out, except last seam in

18 of **B**

Press in

Press out

18 of **Br** — Br is same size and value, start on left

10 of **C**

10 of **Cr** — Cr is same size and value, start on left

6 of **D**

Press in

6 of **E**

6 of **Er** — Er is same size and value, cut opposite direction
E, Er: Press out, last seam in

6 of **F**

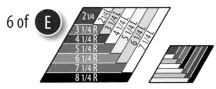

8 of **G**
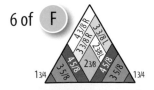

Cut 8       Cut 8

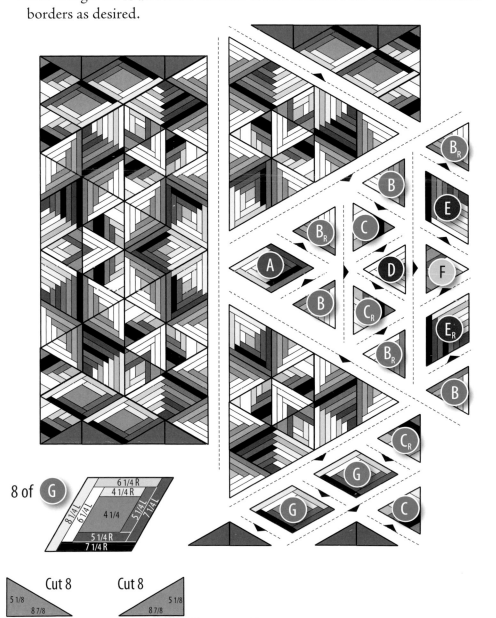

*Chinoiserie*
*Wall Hanging*

**44" x 51"**
Pieced and Machine Quilted
by Linda Tellesbo

47" x 54"

| Fabrics: | Yards: |
|---|---|
| Light | 2 |
| Medium | 1 1/2 |
| Dark | 1 |

Again, simplicity produces a strong design. Linda uses repetition of same-color strips to create solid areas of saturated color and high contrast. The jagged edges and unique shapes of an isometric log cabin design are very evident in this dark snowflake. Additional depth and detail is created on the glowing red center star by the addition of swirling and expanding quilting lines. One of these large blocks makes a great wall hanging or table centerpiece for Christmas or anytime.

- See general directions, pgs. 8-32, for cutting, piecing, and pressing.
- Make quantity of blocks listed using 1½" wide strips for logs. Use 2½" strips for 4¾" log in C.
- Note that C has an overlap at the bottom, center point.
- Make 6 wedges, each wedge has 1 A, 2 B's, 2 Br's, 2 C's, and 1 D.
- Sew wedges three and three and sew across middle to complete the top. To square the quilt top, see pages 20 & 35. Add borders as desired.

6 of **A**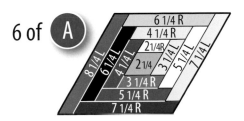

Press out, except last seam in

12 of **B**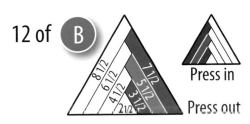

Press in

Press out

12 of **Br** Br is same size and value, except start on left

12 of **C**

6 of **D**

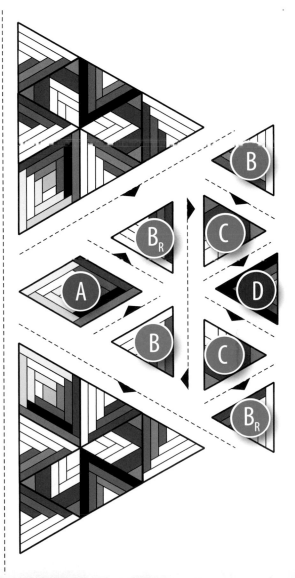

*Chrysanthemum*
**66" x 90"**
Pieced by Sara Nephew,
Machine Quilted by Judy Irish

# Chrysanthemum

**62" x 90"**

Reproduction fabrics with medium to small prints create an antique look that softens the overall effect, a favourite with many quilters. This large block is pieced in both negative and positive to create a design with echoing and connecting elements. All cloth provided by Windham Fabrics.

- See general directions, pgs. 8-32, for cutting, piecing, and pressing.
- Make quantity of blocks listed using 1½" wide strips for logs.
- Make 18 light wedges, each wedge has 1 A and 2 B's.
- Make 18 dark wedges, each wedge has 1 A and 2 C's.
- Make 6 light and 6 dark half-blocks with 3 wedges each. Choose pressing, pg. 34.
- Sew into rows as shown, placing B and setting triangles at ends. Add borders as desired.

| Fabrics: | Yards: |
|----------|--------|
| Chimney | 3/4 |
| Light | 4 |
| Dark | 3 3/4 |

**36 of** Ⓐ

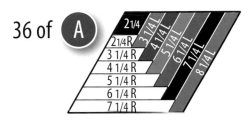

Press out

**44 of** Ⓑ

Press out, except for 18 blocks, press last seam in, Bi

**36 of** Ⓒ

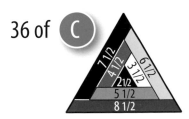

Press out

Cut 8

5 1/8

8 7/8

Cut 8

5 1/8

8 7/8

*Chrysanthemum*
*Wall Hanging*
**31" x 36"**
Pieced by Sara Nephew,
Machine quilted by Judy Irish

# Chrysanthemum Wall Hanging

## 31" x 36"

| Fabrics: | Yards: |
|----------|--------|
| Light | 3/4 |
| Dark | 3/4 |

Sara found a sample swatch book of kimono brocades (polyester, hand woven on silk loom at $115 per yard) and had to try them on this small piece. Even though she sewed the strips onto a foundation, the fabrics tried to wriggle in every direction and pull out of their seams. A final net of machine quilting was needed to catch them all securely. But it's all worth it to see the beautiful fabric patterns and metallic luster of this medallion. A single block of this large pattern makes a great wall hanging or table centerpiece.

+ See general directions, pgs. 8-32, for cutting, piecing, and pressing.
+ Make quantity of blocks listed using 1½" wide strips for logs.
+ Make 6 wedges, each wedge has 1 A and 2 B's.
+ Make 2 half-blocks with 3 wedges each.
+ Cut corner pieces square to grain from 9⅝" strip or sew a 40" long strip set with one 3¾" and three 2¼" strips, as shown. Cut out the two corners noting that the angles are opposite.
+ Add corner pieces. Sew halves together as shown.

6 of **A**

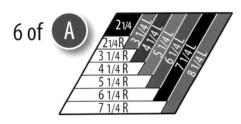

Press out

12 of **B**

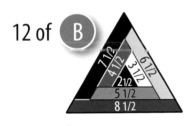

Press out

Cut 1     Cut 1

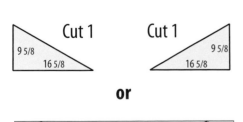

**or**

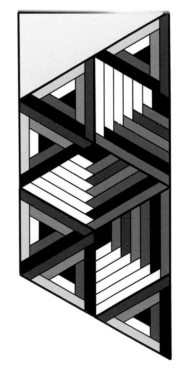

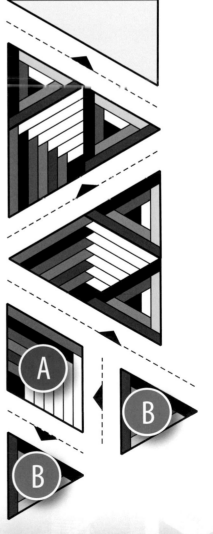

*Dawn Star*
**79" x 91"**
Pieced by Marci Baker

# Dawn Star

**78" x 90"**

| Fabrics: | Yards: |
|---|---|
| Light | 2 3/4 |
| Medium | 3 1/2 |
| Dark | 3 1/4 |

This amazing fabric hexagon seems translucent, as if it were made of glass. In some areas colors are close in value, creating radiance, while in other places high contrast makes the design pop. Marci used almost all solids or batiks, creating the only texture with the jagged edges and sharp lines of the log cabin strips. Notice the pink line running back and forth against the chartreuse, sometimes continuing in the maroon. She planned this quilt as a hexagon to display on her queen-sized bed.

- See general directions, pgs. 8-32, for cutting, piecing, and pressing.
- Make quantity of blocks listed using 1½" wide strips for logs.
- Make 6 wedges, each wedge has 1 A, 2 B's, 3 C's, 4 D's, and 5 E's. Note that the seams between C and D blocks are not supposed to match.
- In the layout, alternate wedges based on direction of pressing of A.
- Sew into halves then join down middle.
- If desired, square quilt by adding setting triangles. See pages 20 & 35 for directions on measuring and cutting these. Add borders as desired.

**6 of** Ⓐ

Press 3 in, 3 out

**12 of** Ⓑ

Press out

**18 of** Ⓒ

Press out

**24 of** Ⓓ

Press 18 out, 6 in, Di

**30 of** Ⓔ

Press out

*Cock's Walk*
**64" x 75"**
Pieced by Linda DeGaeta
Machine Quilted by Janice Jamison

# Dogwood Star

**54" x 62"**

Linda made three of these quilts to help Sara find the best math for putting all the pieces together. What a test! Linda loves adding stacked repeats to many of her quilts, using a focus fabric. Thus the tiny rooster from the border fabric is in the chimneys, and gives the quilt its name. And the surrounding stars have beautiful concentric designs. As always, a smashing quilt.

- See general directions, pgs. 8-32, for cutting, piecing, and pressing.
- Make quantity of blocks listed using 1½" wide strips for logs.
- Piece six star diamonds, each diamond has 1 A, 2 B's, and 1 C.
- Measure the six star diamonds to verify cutting size for setting stars, and setting triangles. See page 37 for details. Make 8 setting stars.
- Alternating direction of pressing for A combine setting stars with star diamonds and setting triangles into center or corner wedges. Work from inner to outer point of star diamonds. The setting star may extend past the edge of the star diamond. This will overlap the corner of another setting star to add float space around the log cabin star.
- Sew the wedges three and three, and then sew across middle to complete the top. Add borders as desired.

| Fabrics: | Yards: |
|----------|--------|
| Light | 2 |
| Medium | 1 1/4 |
| Dark | 1 1/2 |
| Background | 2 |

6 of **A**

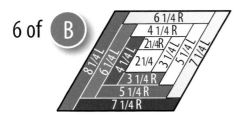

Press 3 in, 3 out

6 of **B**

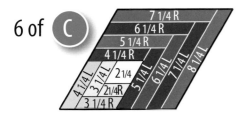

Press out

6 of **C**

Press out except last seam in

48 of **D**

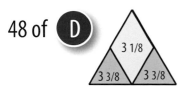

Press left out, right in

Cut 24

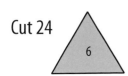

Cut 4     Cut 4

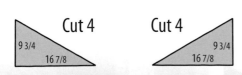

*Eagle's Wings*

**44" x 67"**

Pieced by Sara Nephew

## 39" x 67"

| Fabrics: | Yards: |
| --- | --- |
| Sky | 2 3/4 |
| Black | 1 |
| White | 3/4 |
| Red – Blue | 3/8 each |

This pattern makes so many connections from patriotic feelings to even religious references. The line from the song, "and He will bear me up on eagle's wings" kept repeating in Sara's mind as she sewed and pressed. Sara's husband is Native American and so has a special regard for this magnificent bird. It was fun to choose patriotic fabrics for the finish, and many blue and pink batiks to make up the sky.

+ See general directions, pgs. 8-32, for cutting, piecing, and pressing.
+ Make quantity of blocks listed using 1½" wide strips for logs.
+ Because almost all the diamond blocks have a reverse, you can cut them from folded fabric strips, thereby cutting both blocks at one time.
+ For stripped triangles and diamonds, cut (18) 1½" strips, (2) 1⅜" strips, and (4) 1⅝" strips. Sew into sets as shown, pressing one way.
+ Cut 8¼" diamonds from strip set with 1⅜" strips.
+ Cut 8¾" triangles from strip set with 1⅝" strips. Trim off ¼" from bottom of triangle to make 8½" triangles.
+ Trim any black seam tips that may shadow through white fabric.
+ Lay out blocks with direction of seams opposing when possible. Sew into rows as shown. Join rows to complete top. Add borders as desired.

**6 of A** — Press in / Press out
3 w/o white
3 w/ white

**6 of A_R** — A_R is same size and value, cut opposite direction
3 w/white
3 w/o white

**6 of B** — Press in / Press out

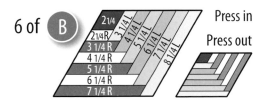

**4 of B_n** — B_n is same size and value, cut opposite direction

**6 of C**

**4 of C_R** — C_R is same size and value, add CW

**3 of 42"**

1 set w/ 1 3/8"     2 sets w/ 1 5/8"

**2 of D** — Use 1 3/8"

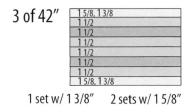

**1 of D_R** — D_R is cut opposite angle

Cut 5     Cut 5

**14 of E** — Use 1 5/8"

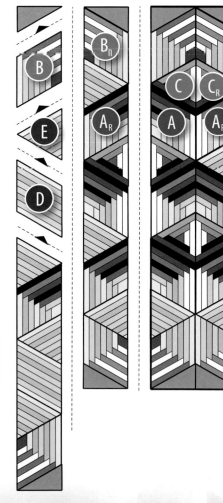

*Fire Garden*

**61" x 79"**

Pieced by Scott Hansen

Quilted by Judy Irish

# Fireworks

## 54" x 72"

This delectable concoction combines multiple colors and busy patterns like fireworks bursting on the 4th of July. Scott assembled these floral fabric gems resembling an English garden gone wild in the heat of the summer. This combination reminds us of a mineral under a microscope, with flashing reflections and jagged connections. Close study repays the viewer with subtleties of color, value, and pattern that are very satisfying and yet captures the excitement of the design.

- See general directions, pgs. 8-32, for cutting, piecing, and pressing.
- Make quantity of blocks listed using 1½" wide strips for logs.
- Make 17 half-blocks with 3 A's each and 18 half-blocks with 3 B's each. Choose pressing, pg. 34.
- Lay out half-blocks and setting triangles. Sew in rows as shown.
- Add borders as desired.

| Fabrics: | Yards: |
|----------|--------|
| Light | 1 5/8 |
| Medium | 3 1/4 |
| Dark | 1 1/8 |

**51 of**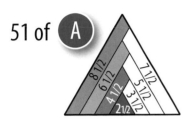

Press left side out, right side in

**54 of**

Press left side out, right side in

Cut 7     Cut 7

5 1/8    8 7/8      5 1/8    8 7/8

*Baby Genius*

**46" x 56"**

Pieced by Sara Nephew,
Machine quilted by Judy Irish

## 47" x 54"

| Fabrics: | Yards: |
|----------|--------|
| Light | 1 3/4 |
| Medium | 1 3/4 |
| Dark | 1 1/2 |

This quilt is designed to catch the eye with all these bright colors and graphic designs. The result is so lively perhaps it's not a quilt for sleeping under. Maybe it's more suitable as a wall hanging to brighten up a child's room or even a whole house. It works! All fabric is from Benartex and the quilt was named after the "Baby Genius" fabric line which was used.

+ See general directions, pgs. 8-32, for cutting, piecing, and pressing.
+ Make quantity of blocks listed using 1½" wide strips for logs.
+ Make 6 wedges, each wedge has 1 A, 1 B, 1 Br, and 3 C's.
+ Alternating direction of pressing for A, sew the wedges three and three and sew across the middle to complete the center hexagon.
+ Square off corners with setting triangles. See pages 20 & 35 for measuring and cutting details. To make the striped version shown in Baby Genius, add one border (green 2½" cut strips) to all four sides. Trim ends. Either cut the setting triangles from strips sets as shown or beginning with a strip that is at least 29" long, add progressively shorter strips until at least 12½" finished width has been added at each corner. Square the quilt top.

6 of **A**

71/4 R · 61/4 R · 51/4 R · 41/4 R · 31/4 R · 21/4 R · 21/4 · 31/4 · 41/4 · 51/4 · 61/4 L · 71/4 L · 81/4 L

Press 3 in, 3 out

6 of **B**

21/4 · 21/4 R · 31/4 R · 41/4 R · 51/4 R · 61/4 R · 71/4 R · 31/4 L · 41/4 L · 51/4 L · 61/4 L · 71/4 L · 81/4 L

Press in          Press out

6 of **Br** — Br is same size and value, cut opposite direction

18 of **C**

61/2 · 71/2 · 31/2 · 41/2 · 21/2 · 51/2 · 81/2

Press out, except last seam in for 6 blocks, Ci

Cut 2          Cut 2

14 1/8 · 24 3/8          14 1/8 · 24 3/8

Or: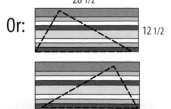

28 1/2          12 1/2

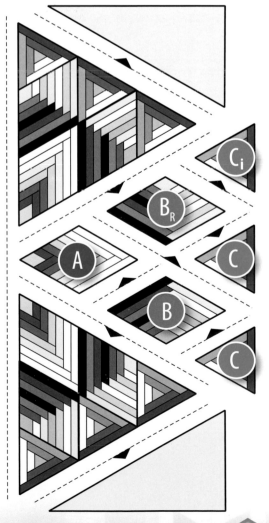

*Flower Petal*

**60" x 70"**

Pieced and Machine Quilted

by Linda Tellesbo

# Flower Petal

## 62" x 72"

Do you like a flower garden? Linda does, and perhaps that's why she chose this pattern and built a bouquet of impressive blooms. Graduated shades of purple make the flowers open wider. The design is made more effective with the light outline around every whole or partial flower. The green grass peeking between the blossoms looks like a summer lawn, carrying out the imaginative effect. These flowers are talking to you!

- See general directions, pgs. 8-32, for cutting, piecing, and pressing, especially for winged triangles and sandwich pieced chimneys, page 32.
- Make quantity of blocks listed using 1½" wide strips for diamond logs.
- If not strip piecing winged triangles, use 2½" wide strips for triangle log. Note that the wings overlap at the base of the triangle B.
- Make 24 wedges, each wedge has 1 A and 2 B's. Alternating direction of pressing for A, use 3 wedges each to make 8 half-blocks. Choose pressing, pg. 34. Make 4 setting triangles from 4 B's.
- Piece together 6 wedges, 1 setting triangle, and 2 B's, and 4 background setting triangles into the large unit as shown. Make 4 of these units.
- Sew into rows and sew rows together to make quilt top. Add borders as desired.

| Fabrics: | Yards: |
|----------|--------|
| Light | 2 1/4 |
| Medium | 3 1/4 |
| Dark | 2 3/4 |

24 of **A**

Press 12 in, 12 out

72 of **B**

Press 36 in, B$_i$, 36 out, B$_o$

Cut 8 — 5 1/8, 8 7/8

Cut 8 — 5 1/8, 8 7/8

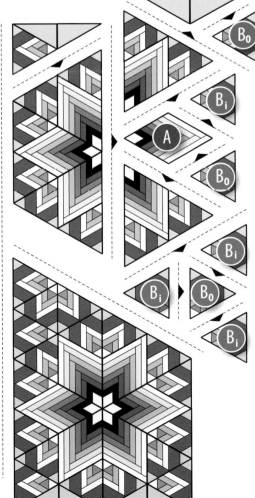

Crystal Blue Persuasion

**60" x 71"**

Pieced by Janet Goad
Machine Quilted by
Linda Daughetee

# *Frost*

**47" x 54"**

The sparkling snow-topped mountains angling across the horizon with grading and contrasting shades and tints of blue, add depth to this unusual landscape. Janet used lots of frosted fabrics in her version of the Frost pattern. The amazingly detailed quilting in the wide white border is almost like snow sculpture. The quilt is named after the song Crystal Blue Persuasion by Tommy James and the Shondells.

- See general directions, pgs. 8-32, for cutting, piecing, and pressing.
- Make quantity of blocks listed using 1½" wide strips for logs.
- Make 6 wedges, each wedge has 1 A, 1 B, 1 Br, 2 C's, and 1 D.
- Make 4 corner units, each unit has 1 D, 1 E, and 3 background setting triangles. Note 2 are mirror image.
- Alternating direction of pressing for A, sew wedges together three and three and sew across the middle to complete the center hexagon. Add corner units.
- Add borders as desired. Janet used a 1½"-cut inner border and a 7"-cut outer border.

| Fabrics: | Yards: |
|----------|--------|
| Light | 2 1/4 |
| Medium | 1 1/4 |
| Dark | 1 1/4 |

**6 of (A)**
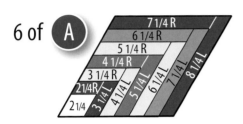
Press 3 in, 3 out

**12 of (B)**
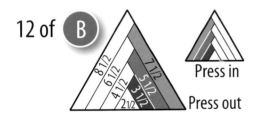
Press in
Press out

**12 of (Br)** Br is same size and value, start on left side

**12 of (C)**

**12 of (D)**

**6 of (E)**
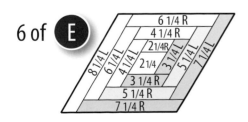

**Cut 6** (5 1/8, 8 7/8)  **Cut 6** (5 1/8, 8 7/8)

*Sunshine Came Softly*
**68" x 76"**
Pieced by Linda DeGaeta
Machine Quilted by Janice Jamison

# Frost Star

**62" x 72"**

It's truly surprising to view what Linda has done with the Frost Star pattern, she using large colorful prints to obtain a quilt saturated with color and texture. These large prints by Kaffe Fassett make the quilt look almost fizzy creating a magical effect. Consider how different this quilt would look using fabric selections similar to the related pattern Frost.

- See general directions, pgs. 8-32, for cutting, piecing, and pressing.
- Make quantity of blocks listed using 1½" wide strips for logs.
- Recommend selecting fabrics as you make the blocks and build outwards, adjusting choices as you go.
- Make 6 wedges from 1 A, 1 B, 1 C, 1 Cri, 2 D's. Alternating direction of pressing for A, Sew wedges three and three then through middle for center star.
- Make 20 half hexagons with 1 B, 1 C, and 1 Cr. Using 12 of these, F, and Fr, make 6 flat pyramid units. Add to top and bottom of center star.
- Make 4 corner units (2 are mirror image) with 1 flat pyramid, 2 half-hexagons, 1 B, 2 E's, and 3 background setting triangles. On two, add 1 E and 4 setting triangles. Add corner units as shown. Add borders as desired.

| Fabrics: | Yards: |
|---|---|
| Light | 3 |
| Medium | 1 1/2 |
| Dark | 2 |

**6 of**

Press 3 in, 3 out

**30 of**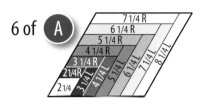

**26 of**

Press 6 in, 20 out

Press out

**26 of**  Cr is same size and value, except start on right

**12 of**

**10 of**

**6 of**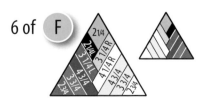

**6 of** Fr is same size and value, cut opposite direction

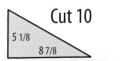 Cut 10

5 1/8

8 7/8

 Cut 10

5 1/8

8 7/8

*Frosty Windows*
**74" x 89"**
Pieced by Bobbie Crosby
Machine Quilted by Linda Dunlap

# Frosty Windows

## 62" x 77"

A symphony of soft colors with a misty look has a pastel hint here and there. Somehow it looks like a scene from nature, bushes with large beautiful flowers. The dark hexagons are composed of six triangles, providing an opportunity to use stacked repeats if a quilter wished for a design challenge.

- See general directions, pgs. 8-32, for cutting, piecing, and pressing, especially for winged triangles, page 31.
- Make quantity of blocks listed using 1½" wide strips for logs.
- If using stacked repeats*, layout before assembling, to your satisfaction.
- Note that the winged triangles have an overlap at the bottom center.
- Sew 32 half-blocks with 3 A's each. Choose pressing, pg. 34. Make 16 end units from 2 A's each.
- Sew into rows as shown. Add borders as desired.

| Fabrics: | Yards: |
|---|---|
| Light | 2 1/4 |
| Medium | 3/4 |
| Dark | 3 1/2 |

128 of

Press left wing in, right wing out

Cut 8    Cut 8

5 1/8    5 1/8
8 7/8    8 7/8

*See Doubledipity by Sara Nephew for more information on stacked repeats

*Glory*

**73" x 82"**

Pieced by Diane Coombs

Machine Quilted by Judy Irish

# Glory

62" x 72"

Glory, Glory, Hallelujah! Diane chose patriotic colors and strong contrasts to bring out the best in this log cabin quilt. Then she stacked a dainty floral print so she would have pretty concentric patterns in the bold white stars. The unusual yellow chimney diamonds add expanding movement and a golden gleam to the whole design.

- See general directions, pgs. 8-32, for cutting, piecing, and pressing, especially for winged triangles, page 31.
- Make quantity of blocks listed using 2½" wide strips for A logs and 1½" for all others.
- Make 12 half-blocks with 3 A's each.
- Make 6 wedges, each wedge has 1 A, 1 B, 2 C's, 1 D, 2 E's, and 2 half-blocks. Sew wedges three and three, then seam down center.
- Make 4 corner units from 1 D, 4 F's, and 4 background setting triangles. Join to center. Add borders as desired.

| Fabrics: | Yards: |
|---|---|
| Light | 1 3/4 |
| Medium | 2 1/4 |
| Dark | 2 3/4 |

42 of **A**

Press left in, right out

6 of **B**

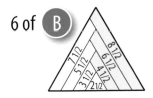

12 of **C**

Press out, except last seam in

10 of **D**

12 of **E**

16 of **F**

Cut 8          Cut 8

*Iris*

**80" x 98"**

Pieced by Diane Coombs

Machine Quilted by Becky Marshall

# Iris

62" x 81"

Fun with flowers! Build your blooms from strips of purple, blue, lavender, maroon, yellow, gold, and green fabrics. Diane even made a yellow flower that disappears. But everyone told her to put it in anyway, a more old-fashioned approach. Now some ladies have said it's their favorite flower. Diane added the iris border on pg. 112 for a petal-shaped finish to this pretty quilt.

| Fabrics: | Yards: |
| --- | --- |
| Light | 3 3/4 |
| Medium | 1/2 |
| Dark | 3 1/2 |

- See general directions, pgs. 8-32, for cutting, piecing, and pressing.
- Make quantity of blocks listed using 1½" wide strips for logs.
- For stripped triangles, cut (18) 1½" strips and (6) 1⅝" strips. Sew 3 sets of (6) 1½" with 1⅝" on either side. Press seams for half the strip one way, the other half the opposite so that seams can oppose.
- From the strip sets, cut 8¾" triangles. Trim off ¼" from bottom of triangle to make 8½" triangles. Top and bottom strips will be narrower than other strips.
- Assemble blocks and setting triangles into 4 left and four right vertical rows. Begin at the bottom for lefts and at the top for rights if following pressing directions.
- Sew rows together and add borders as desired.

48 of (A)

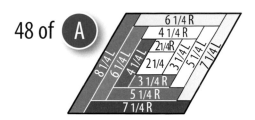

12 of (B)

12 of (B<sub>R</sub>)   B<sub>R</sub> is same size and value, start on left side, add CW

3 of 42"

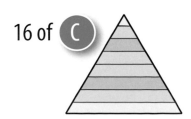

16 of (C)

Cut 8     Cut 8

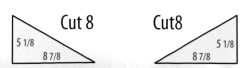

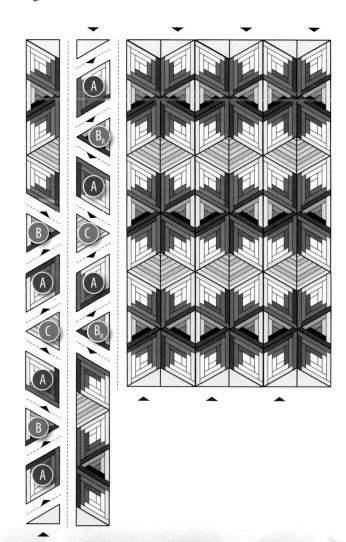

*Fuchsias*
**61" x 70"**
Pieced by Sara Nephew,
Machine quilted by Judy Irish

# Mexican Star

**54" x 62"**

The Fuchsias quilt is saturated with shades of purple and pink, just like the flowers that inspired the fabric design. Little leaves and dangling flowers add delicate details to this strong overall design. Hummingbirds love fuchsias, so this star is surrounded by busy little quilted birds, avian acrobats. All the fabric is from the Fuchsia Fabric Collection by Maywood Studio.

- See general directions, pgs. 8-32, for cutting, piecing, and pressing, especially for winged triangles, C, page 31.
- Make quantity of blocks listed using 1½" wide strips for all logs except 2½" wide strips for wings of C.
- Make 6 wedges each with 1 A and 2 B's. Make 6 wedges each with 1 A, 1 C, and 1 Cʀ.
- Measure the height of your wedges to be sure these next pieces will fit. See page 35 for guidance. Adjust measurements in next steps accordingly.
- Make (4) 16" x 19" rectangles with border strip. Cut corner sections, 2 with left end cut off at 30° angle, and 2 with right end cut off.
- Sew (4) 16 ¼" x 42" border strips. Cut (8) 16 ¼" triangles.
- Add corners and triangles to edges. Start seams inside and work toward outer edge. To make the star float similar to Sara's Fuchsias, make the strips wider and longer by similar amounts, trimming excess from sides.
- Assemble as shown in diagram. Trim sides straight. Add borders as desired.

| Fabrics: | Yards: |
|---|---|
| Light | 1 1/4 |
| Medium | 3/4 |
| Dark | 1 1/4 |
| Background* | 2 1/2 |

*If no border is used, need twelve 20" lengths of 5-8" border print. Determine yardage using this info and the repeat of the border fabric.

**12 of**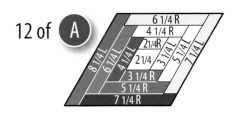

**12 of**

Press last two seams in for 6, out for 6.

**6 of**

**6 of**  Cʀ is same size and value, except opposite direction

**Cut 2L, 2R**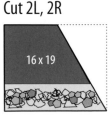

16 x 19

16 x 19

**Cut 8**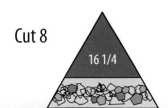

16 1/4

*Sunsets & Stars*
**66" x 74"**
Pieced by Kathie Kryla
Machine Quilted by Judy Irish

# Montana

**54" x 62"**

Purple, blue, pink, and green – Wow! A jewel-toned exploding blossom in the middle of a starry garden. A wreath of flowers twines softly around the center white-tipped hexagon. Somehow a mayfly and hummingbird were quilted in, and Kathie begged for more. It's like a game to see how many little creatures you can find on this quilt.

- See general directions, pgs. 8-32, for cutting, piecing, and pressing.
- Make quantity of blocks listed using 1½" wide strips for logs.
- Assemble six star diamonds, each diamond has 2 A's, 2 B's, and 2 Br's.
- Measure the six star diamonds to verify cutting size for setting stars, and setting triangles. See page 37 for details.
- Make 8 setting stars. Press corner triangle seams out on 4 and in on 4.
- Working from inner to outer point of star diamonds, combine setting stars with star diamonds and setting triangles into center or corner wedges. The setting star may extend past the edge of the star diamond. This will overlap the corner of another setting star to add float space at each point.
- Sew the wedges three and three, and then sew across middle to complete the top. Add borders as desired.

| Fabrics: | Yards: |
|----------|--------|
| Light | 3/4 |
| Medium | 1 1/4 |
| Dark | 1 1/2 |
| Background | 2 |

**12 of A**
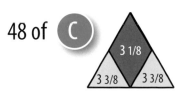
71/4 R / 61/4 R / 51/4 R / 41/4 R / 41/4 / 51/4 L / 61/4 L / 71/4 L / 81/4 L

**12 of B**
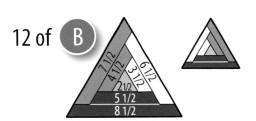
71/2 / 41/2 / 61/2 / 31/2 / 21/2 / 51/2 / 81/2

**12 of Br** — Br is same size and value, start on left side, add CW.

**48 of C**

3 1/8 / 3 3/8 / 3 3/8

Press left out, right in

**Cut 24**

6

**Cut 4** / **Cut 4**

9 3/4 / 16 7/8 — 9 3/4 / 16 7/8

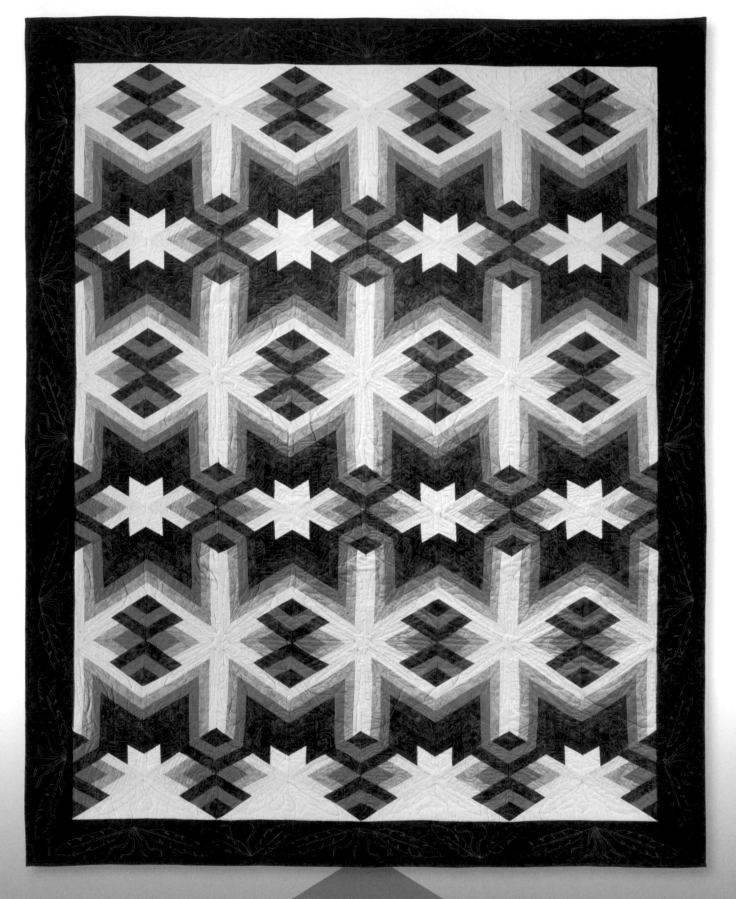

*Native Blanket*

**65" x 82"**

Pieced by Bonnie Walker

Machine Quilted by Sheila Crum

# Native Blanket

62" x 72"

The color palette emphasizes the look of a Native American design in this quilt. Actually, the colors are limited to brown, black, and white, but because of the use of graded shades and tints, the design looks very colorful. Less is more! This quilt would be perfect, a standout, in a hunting cabin or ski lodge. Bonnie splits her time between Texas and Alaska, so that may have influenced her choice to make this design that captures the Native American spirit.

- See general directions, pgs. 8-32, for cutting, piecing, and pressing, especially for winged triangles, page 32.
- Make the quantity of blocks listed using 1½" wide strips for logs.
- Assemble blocks and setting triangles into 4 left and four right vertical rows, placing A's pressed in for left rows and A's pressed out for right rows. When joining blocks into rows begin at the bottom for lefts and at the top for rights.
- Sew rows together and add borders as desired.

| Fabrics: | Yards: |
|---|---|
| Light | 3 |
| Medium | 2 1/4 |
| Dark | 2 1/4 |

40 of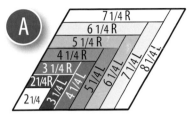

Press 20 in, 20 out

48 of

Press wings, left out, right in

Cut 8          Cut 8

*Ornament*

**58" x 65"**

Pieced by Kathy Syring

Machine Quilted by Judy Irish

# Ornament

**47" x 54"**

| Fabrics: | Yards: |
|----------|--------|
| Light | 3/4 |
| Medium | 1 1/4 |
| Dark | 1 1/4 |
| Background | 1 |

Again, a simplified palette can have a striking effect. It has the look of a stained glass window. Kathy was consistent throughout with the order of her fabric placement, and the result is a very strong design in a complementary color scheme, orange and blue. The dark strips outline the basic structure of the design, and make the lighter colors glow. The printed pattern in the dark border and fill-in pieces add an impression of a velvety texture.

+ See general directions, pgs. 8-32, for cutting, piecing, and pressing.
+ Make quantity of blocks listed using 1½" wide strips for logs.
+ Make 6 wedges, each wedge has 3 A's and 3 B's. The center A will be pressed in for 3, and out for 3.
+ Alternating direction of pressing for center A's, join wedges three and three and sew across the middle.
+ Measure the wedges and verify cutting sizes are correct for corner setting triangles. See page 35 for details.
+ Add corner pieces. Add borders as desired.

18 of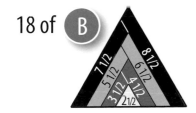

Press 9 in, 9 out

18 of (B)

Cut 2

Cut 2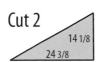

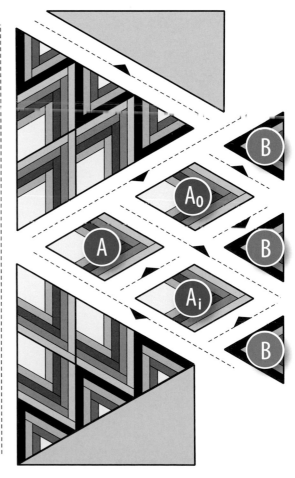

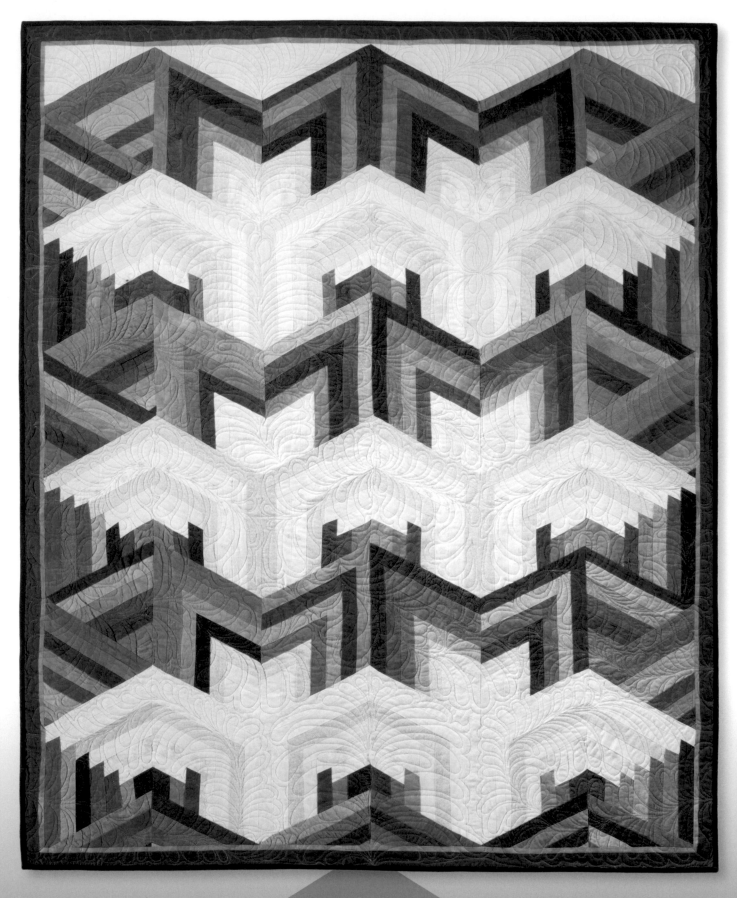

*Owls*

**46" x 55"**

Pieced by Joan Dawson

Quilted by Jeanne Rumans

# Owls

## 47" x 59"

Owls are a favorite animal motif of many people. The owl can be a symbol of the supernatural or of wisdom. But to many, it's just a cute bird, with its big round eyes. Joan pieced the background in many colors; jewel-tones, shades, and pastels. This adds a lively stripe behind the ghostly fliers. The free-form quilting pattern of all-over feathers is a perfect curvy counterpoint for these geometric shapes.

+ See general directions, pgs. 8-32, for cutting, piecing, and pressing.
+ Make quantity of blocks listed using 1½" wide strips for logs.
+ For stripped triangles, cut (18) 1½" strips and (6) 1⅝" strips. Sew 3 sets of (6) 1½" with 1⅝" on either side. seams for one half strip one way, the other half the opposite so that seams can oppose.
+ From the strip sets, cut 8¾" triangles. Trim off ¼" from bottom of triangle to make 8½" triangles. Top and bottom strips will be narrower than other strips.
+ Assemble blocks and setting triangles into six vertical rows, beginning at the bottom for those with seams pressed up and at the top for those with seams pressed down.
+ Sew rows together and add borders as desired.

| Fabrics: | Yards: |
|---|---|
| Owls | 1 3/4 |
| Background | 2 1/2 |

12 of **A**

Press 6 in, 6 out

3 of **B**     Press in

Press out

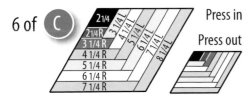

3 of **Bᵣ**    Bᵣ is same size and value, cut opposite direction

6 of **C**     Press in

Press out

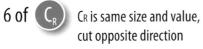

6 of **Cᵣ**    Cᵣ is same size and value, cut opposite direction

3 of 42"

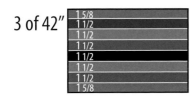

12 of **D**

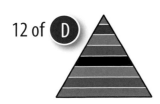

Cut 6          Cut 6

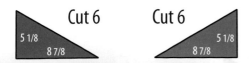

5 1/8     8 7/8          8 7/8     5 1/8

*Painted Desert*

**70" x 70"**

Pieced by Kathy Syring

Machine Quilted by Judy Irish

# Painted Desert

62" x 63"

Kathy used colors reminiscent of Native American art to create a strongly masculine design for her son's bed. The unusual quilting pattern, a mosaic-like web of straight lines and sharp corners, evokes images from the desert, with cliff walls, colorful rocks, grooves and cracks in the stones. Consistent use of color with little variation creates an ancient-looking medallion inset with mineral colors like turquoise, jasper, flint, and agate.

- See general directions, pgs. 8-32, for cutting, piecing, and pressing, especially for winged triangle, A, page 32.
- Make quantity of blocks listed using 1½" wide strips for logs.
- Make 6 wedges, each wedge has 1 A, 1 B, 2 C's, and 3 D's, pressed out. Make 6 subunits with 2 C's and 1 D, pressed in.
- Alternating direction of pressing for A, sew the wedges three and three. Do not sew these half-hexagons together yet. Add a subunit to the outer edge of each half hexagon.
- With the other 4 subunits, remaining C's, and two sizes of setting triangles, make 4 corner sections. Two are mirror image.
- Add corner units to each half-hexagon and sew these two halves together. Add borders as desired.

| Fabrics: | Yards: |
|----------|--------|
| Light | 2 1/4 |
| Medium | 1 1/4 |
| Dark | 2 1/4 |
| Background | 1 |

6 of

Press 3 in, 3 out

6 of

Press 3 in, 3 out

28 of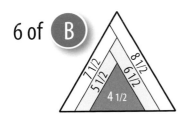

24 of

Press 6 in, Di, 18 out

Cut 2   Cut 2
5 1/8   5 1/8
8 7/8   8 7/8

Cut 2   Cut 2
14 1/8   14 1/8
24 3/8   24 3/8

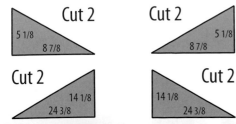

*Lilies in the Valley*
**57" x 62"**
Pieced and Machine Quilted
by Janice Jamison

# Shield

## 47" x 54"

Light, bright colors and strong geometry produce a quilt that exudes happiness. The Shield pattern looks great as a flower, one big flower in the middle with nodding bells all around the outside. The curves of the feather quilting filling the surface of the whole quilt soften the design, bringing thoughts of wrapping up in peaceful bliss.

- See general directions, pgs. 8-32, for cutting, piecing, and pressing.
- Make quantity of blocks listed using 1½" wide strips for logs.
- Make 6 wedges, each wedge has 1 A, 2 B's, and 3 C's. Sew the wedges together three and three and sew across the middle to complete the center hexagon.
- Join 3 D's and 3 setting triangles to make a corner unit. Make 2 and their mirror images. Sew corner units onto center hexagon. Add borders as desired.

| Fabrics: | Yards: |
|----------|--------|
| Light | 1 1/4 |
| Medium | 1 1/2 |
| Dark | 1 3/4 |

6 of A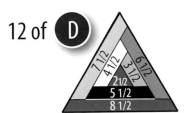

12 of B

Press 6 in, 6 out

18 of C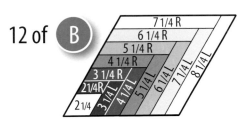

12 of D

Press out, except last seam in on 8

Cut 6

Cut 6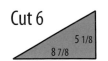

*Snow Stars*

**77" x 92"**

Pieced by Joyce Lawrence Cambron

Machine Quilted by Yvette Ebaugh

# *Star Sampler*

**63" x 81"**

| Fabrics: | Yards: |
|---|---|
| Lg Star Print | 3/4* |
| Light | 1 3/4 |
| Medium | 2 1/4 |
| Dark | 3 1/4 |

*or enough for 6 repeats

Joyce answered the perennial designer's question, "What would happen if…" She used graphic prints and stacked repeats in shades of blue to produce no two snowflakes alike, as in nature. She had fun by playing with design elements in the individual stars, mixing and matching, turning and reversing. Let yourself go! Then Joyce designed the dainty border, Candlestick.

- See general directions, pgs. 8-32, for cutting, piecing, and pressing, especially for winged triangles, and sandwich pieced chimneys, page 31.
- Make quantity of blocks listed using 1½" wide strips for diamond logs and 2½" wide strips for wider winged triangle logs.
- Alternating direction of pressing for A's and D's, sew triangles three and three then down the middle to make each hexagon star. Choose pressing, pg. 34.
- Layout in desired format. Sew setting triangles on opposite sides of each hexagon to make star units.
- Sew star units together in rows. Sew rows together. Add borders as desired. Directions for this pieced border are on page 111.

**24 of**

Press 12 in, 12 out

**18 of** B

Press wings: left out, right in

**24 of** C

Press wings: left in, right out

**30 of** D

Press 15 in, 15 out

**40 of** E

 Cut 8     Cut 8

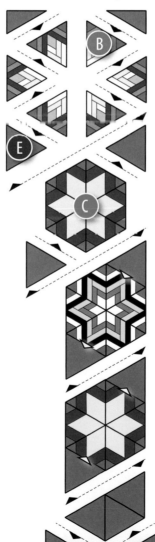

*Winter Nation* II

**72" x 85"**

Pieced by Linda DeGaeta

Machine Quilted by Janice Jamison

# Stripped Stars

## 70" x 86"

Here red, white, and blue go together in an unanticipated way. Linda made an assortment of snowflakes out of shades of blue, opening a window on winter! Some are surprisingly dark. They create a network, a structure that holds the whole picture together. The chimney is always red, a traditional touch. Dark blue also fills in top and bottom and finishes with borders at left and right. For other variations of this pattern, see page 38.

- See general directions, pgs. 8-32, for cutting, piecing, and pressing.
- Make quantity of blocks listed using 1½" wide strips for logs.
- Assemble groups of 3 similar triangles into half-blocks. Choose pressing, page 34.
- Place half-blocks according to the diagram and sew into vertical rows including setting triangles at the ends.
- Sew the rows together and add borders as desired.

| Fabrics: | Yards: |
| --- | --- |
| Chimneys | 3/4 |
| Light | 4 |
| Medium | 1 |
| Dark | 3 1/4 |

54 of **A**

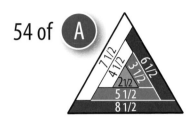

54 of **B**

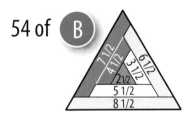

54 of **C**

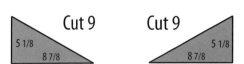

Cut 9          Cut 9

*Tropical Tangerine*

**75" x 85"**

Pieced by Sarah Newman

Machine Quilted by Kim McBride

# *Tropical*

62" x 72"

Can you see the leaves of the palm trees in this design? Perhaps that's why Sarah chose green as a main fabric color in her version of the Tropical pattern. Actually, green and orange is a traditional color scheme, particularly in quilts from the 1930s. A mix of tints and shades of both colors adds interest to the strong four-star layout. Even the border is divided into two colors along the angles of the blocks.

+ See general directions, pgs. 8-32, for cutting, piecing, and pressing.
+ Make quantity of blocks listed using 1½" wide strips for logs.
+ Make 24 Tropical wedges, each wedge has 1 A and 2 B's. Note two wedges with Bi's for opposing seams along center of quilt. Make 4 setting wedges, each wedge has 1 B and 3 Br's.
+ Sew Tropical wedges three and three and then across the middle to complete 4 hexagons.
+ Join 1 hexagon, 1 setting wedge, 2 Br's, and 4 setting triangles to make the unit. Make 4 of these and then sew in pairs to make halves. Assemble the two halves into the top. Add borders as desired.

| Fabrics: | Yards: |
|---|---|
| Chimneys | 1/2 |
| Light | 2 1/2 |
| Medium | 1 3/4 |
| Dark | 1 3/4 |

24 of (A)

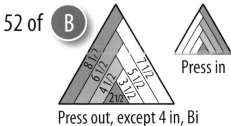

Press light in, dark out

52 of (B)

Press out, except 4 in, Bi

Press in

20 of (Br) Br is same size and value, except start on right

Cut 8

Cut 8

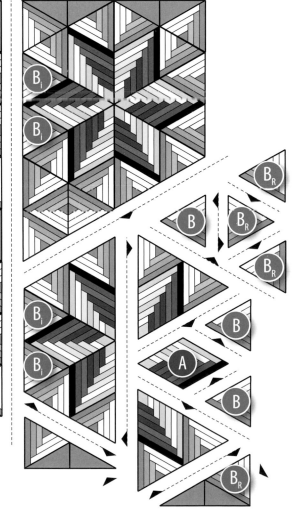

*Calliope*

**76" x 82"**

Pieced by Linda DeGaeta

Machine Quilted by Janice Jamison

# Tulip

62" x 72"

The logs of this quilt make shapes that look like buds and flowers. A cool turquoise background, though bright, recedes and the hotter corals, pinks and yellows come forward, creating a lattice-work of flowers and stars against the blue sky of spring and summer. Linda decided to add a pieced border where the dark lines in the border echo the isometric triangles of the design.

- See general directions, pgs. 8-32, for cutting, piecing, and pressing.
- Make quantity of blocks listed using 1½" wide strips for logs.
- Assemble 6 wedges, each wedge has 2 A's, 2 B's, 2 C's, and 8 D's, each.
- Sew the wedges three and three and sew across the center to complete the hexagon.
- Make 4 corner units, each unit has 1 A, 4 C's, and 4 setting triangles. Two are mirror image of the others.
- Add corner units and then borders as desired.

| Fabrics: | Yards: |
|----------|--------|
| Light | 3 |
| Medium | 2 |
| Dark | 1 1/2 |

16 of **A**

Press out, except last seam in

12 of **B**

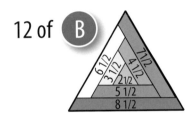

28 of **C**

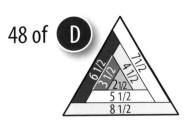

48 of **D**

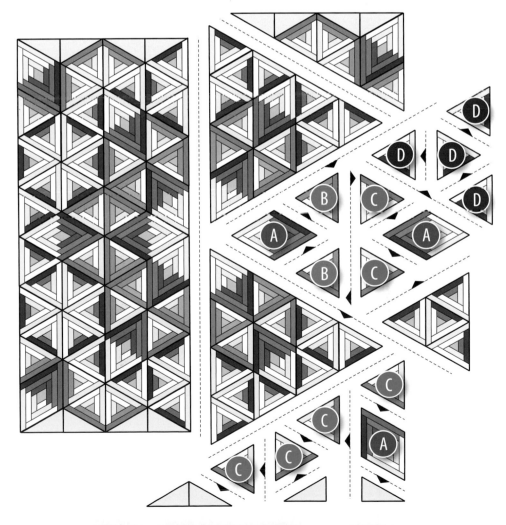

Cut 8    Cut 8

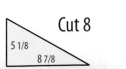
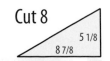

*Tumbling Logs*
**86" x 95"**
Pieced by Terri Shinn
Machine Quilted by Judy Irish

## 70" x 86"

| Fabrics: | Yards: |
|---|---|
| Chimneys | 1/2 |
| Light | 2 1/2 |
| Medium | 2 3/4 |
| Dark | 2 3/4 |
| Background | 3/4 |

Whether you see little houses with rosy windows or big cubes with pink diamonds scattered over all, either way Terri created a graphic queen-sized quilt for her daughter's wedding present. This stunning design uses trendy fabric to update the traditional design. Log strips are sewn together making more solid areas, but the beige and blue create the steps. Huge swirling circles in the border fabric frame the optical illusion of the tumbling blocks. Note that Terri's quilt is larger than the original pattern.

+ See general directions, pgs. 8-32, for cutting, piecing, and pressing.
+ Make quantity of blocks listed using 1½" wide strips for logs.
+ Assemble into left and right half-blocks using 1 A with 1B (press to A), and 1 Aʀ with 1 C, (press to C).
+ Sew half-blocks and setting triangles into vertical rows.
+ Sew the rows together. Add borders as desired.

27 of **A**

Press in

Press out

27 of **Aʀ** Aʀ is same size and value, except start on right

27 of **B**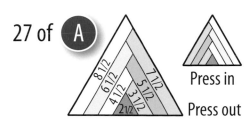

27 of **C**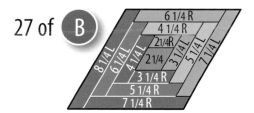

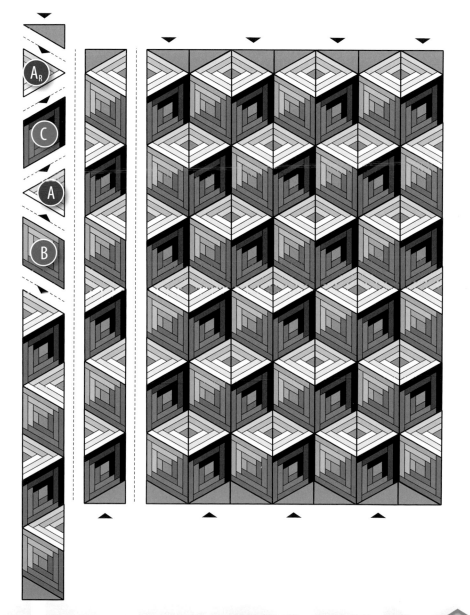

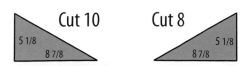

Cut 10          Cut 8

*Will O' Wisp*

**56" x 59"**

Pieced by Kathy Syring

Machine Quilted by Judy Irish

# Will O' Wisp

47" x 54"

It is surprising how dark this quilt really is but the bold yellows, oranges, and reds are visually strong creating a glowing effect. The main fabric in the quilt is a printed ombre which shades from one color to another. All sliced up into strips and sewn back together with other colors added, this produces a flame-like ripple and waver. The warmth and dramatic statement of this design make it a quilt with new impact each time you see it. Don't lay it down on a bed; put it up on the wall, where you can see every part of it.

+ See general directions, pgs. 8-32, for cutting, piecing, and pressing.
+ Make quantity of blocks listed using 1½" wide strips for logs.
+ Make 6 wedges, each wedge has 1 A, 1 B, 2 C's, and 3 D's.
+ Alternating direction of pressing for A, sew the wedges three and three and sew across the middle to complete the hexagon.
+ Make four corner units, each unit has 2 Bʀ's, 1 D, and 3 setting triangles. Two are mirror image of the others.
+ Join corner units and add borders as desired.

| Fabrics: | Yards: |
|----------|--------|
| Light | 1 1/4 |
| Medium | 2 |
| Dark | 1 1/4 |

6 of **A**

Press 3 in, 3 out

6 of **B**

Press in

Press 3 in, 3 out

8 of **Bʀ**  Bʀ is same size and value, except start on right

12 of **C**

22 of **D**

Cut 6    Cut 6

*Winter Snow*

**69" x 76"**

Pieced by Sara Nephew,

Machine quilted by Judy Irish

# Winter Snow

**62" x 72"**

| Fabrics: | Yards: |
|----------|--------|
| Chimneys | 5/8 |
| Light | 3 1/4 |
| Dark | 2 3/4 |

The last quilt in the book is the first quilt Sara made for this book, and it may turn out to be her favorite. Inspired by a decorator swatch book of polished cotton obtained at a garage sale, Sara sorted the solid color swatches into light and dark, adding more from her own fabric library. When the stripped blocks were assembled into a quilt top, these crystalline structures emerged. The quilt called for a pieced border, and the faceted Winding Road pattern on page 114 finished the adventure.

- See general directions, pgs. 8-32, for cutting, piecing, and pressing.
- Make quantity of blocks listed using 1½" wide strips for logs, varying the value of the dark section as shown in the quilt.
- Alternating direction of pressing on last seam, make 40 half-blocks with 3 A's each.
- Assemble half-blocks and setting triangles into vertical rows. Sew rows together.
- Add the Winding Road border, page 114 or add other borders as desired.

**120 of** Ⓐ

Press out, except
last seam in on 60

Cut 8 — 5 1/8 / 8 7/8

Cut 8 — 5 1/8 / 8 7/8

# Borders

## GENERAL BORDER INSTRUCTIONS

To have these pieced borders fit your quilt you will need to measure the top. You will compare this size to the possible sizes of the border based on the design unit. If needed, inner borders will be added to make the top match the pieced borders.

Remember to subtract seam allowances from measured pieces. Then figure the finished sizes, and add seam allowances back.

1. Measure the width and length of the top. This is the unfinished measurement.
**48" x 77" unfinished with 6" unit length**

2. Subtract ½" from each measurement for seam allowance. This is the finished width and length of the top.
**47½" x 76½" finished**

3. Divide both the width and the length by the unit length and round up to the nearest whole number. This is the minimum number of units that will be needed for the top/bottom borders and side borders, respectively. You can make it more than this if it would look better to float the center section more.
**47½" / 6 = 7.833 => 8 units for top and bottom borders.**
**76½" / 6 = 12.667 => 13 units for side borders.**

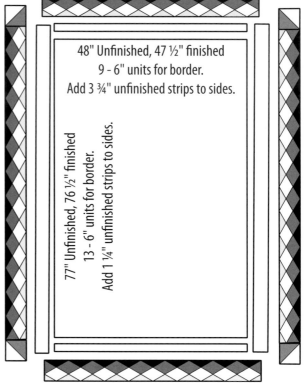

48" Unfinished, 47 ½" finished
9 - 6" units for border.
Add 3 ¾" unfinished strips to sides.

77" Unfinished, 76 ½" finished
13 - 6" units for border.
Add 1 ¼" unfinished strips to sides.

4. To determine width of the float strips, multiply number of units by unit length and subtract the finished size. This difference needs to be divided by two (for borders on both sides) and then ½" added for seam allowances. These strips will be added to the adjacent sides because it is making the width or length of the quilt top fit the border length.

**Side Float Strip** (use top and bottom measurements)
**8 units x 6" = 48". So, 48 – 47½" = ½". Divide by 2 and add seam allowance, ½ / 2 = 1/4.**
**So, ¼ + ½ = ¾ wide float strip. This is such a narrow strip, so add another unit, to make it 9 units which will make the float strip 3 ¾".**

**Top & Bottom Float Strip** (use side measurements)
**13 units x 6" = 78". So, 78 – 76½ = 1½". Divide by 2 and add seam allowance, 1½ / 2 = ¾.**
**So, ¾ + ½ = 1¼" strips will be added to the top and bottom of the quilt to match the length of the side borders.**

5. Before cutting these strips, sew a section of the border and measure to be sure the units measure as expected. Make adjustments if needed.

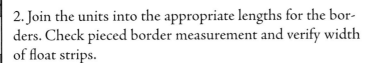

## CANDLESTICK BORDER

Finished Unit Size: 5¾" x 5"

Determine number of units needed for quilt. Add extra background triangles for squaring off ends.

For each unit needed cut the shapes shown in the diagram.

For number of shapes per 40" strip, see exploded view.

1. Piece the units together by sewing the triangles onto the diamond, the log onto this unit, then the small triangles onto the corners. Finally add the largest triangle onto one side, being consistent on which side.

2. Join the units into the appropriate lengths for the borders. Check pieced border measurement and verify width of float strips.

3. Add float strips as needed.

4. For corners, add 5½" background squares to side borders.

5. Add pieced borders to quilt top to finish the design.

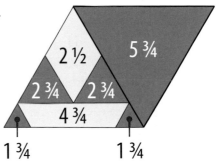

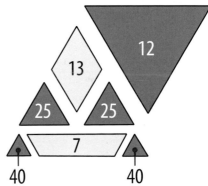

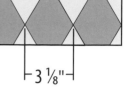

## Iris Border

Finished Unit Size: 3⅛" x 4⅛"
Number of units from 40-45" sets: 9-10
Determine number of units needed for the sides. Add 8 for trimming ends, and as an option, add 4 for corner units.

For each strip set, cut strips:
(1) 3¼" iris fabric
(1) 2⅛" background fabric
(1) 3½" background fabric

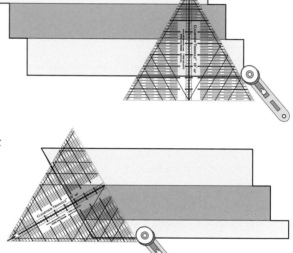

1. Sew strips together lengthwise, with iris fabric in the middle, staggering each strip by 2" or so. Press toward the darker fabric. At right end of strip cut 60° angle.

2. Turn fabric and position ruler at left end. Cut 3¼" slices.

3. With each slice narrow strip down, align ruler point down, with 1⅞" rule line at seam. Cut off triangle section (has two fabric pieces.)

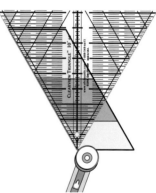

4. Turn the slice around, align ruler point down, with 3¼" rule line at seam. Cut off triangle.

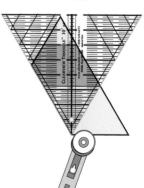

Use these and triangles from Step 3 for piecing on the quilt back or for another quilt.

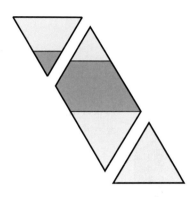

5. Lay out units and sew together. Check border length and make sure float strips are correct size. Square ends of borders.

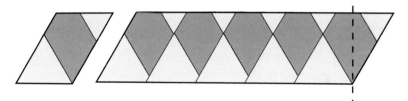

6. Add float strips on each side as needed. Add top and bottom borders.

7. For corners, either use 4⅝" squares of background or add pieces of background to cone units so the piece can be trimmed to a 4⅝" square. See corner unit for general position of pieces.

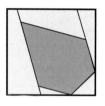

8. Add corners to side borders. Add side borders to quilt top.

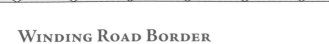

6"

## WINDING ROAD BORDER

A great finish that adds that extra special touch making the central design float.
Unit length: 6"
Number of units from 40" length: 10

Determine number of units required for each border. Add 2 extra for each border to allow for trimming. Take total number of units needed for all 4 borders, divide by 10 to determine number of sets to make and yardage required.

For each strip set cut:
(2) 3½" strips of light
(1) 3½" strip of dark
(1) 3½" strip of background

1. Sew sets with light, light, dark, and background, staggering each strip by 2" or so. Using a long ruler and the 60 degree ruler, cut the 60 degree angle as shown.

2. Turn the strip with angled end to the left. Align 3½" along the angled edge. Check the angle with the 60 degree ruler as shown. Remove 60 degree ruler and cut along right side of long ruler. Cut number of sections needed.

3. Sew the 3½" sections together as shown, aligning the diamond points. Trim long edges to ¼" beyond the diamond points. The border should measure close to 5¾" but not exactly.

4. Double check your border sizes with the sewn borders that you have made. Adjust float strip size if needed. Add the top and bottom border to the quilt.

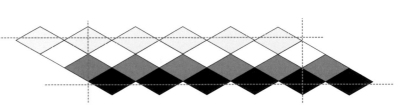

5. Complete the side borders with corners. Make 4 half square triangle squares using 6⅛" squares, 2 dark and 2 background. Cut on one diagonal, sew in pairs, and add to ends of side borders. Add side borders to complete your top.

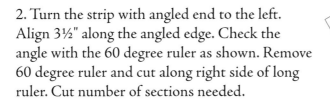

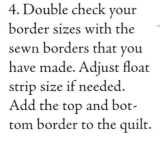

# Sara Nephew

Sara Nephew is a quilt designer, author, teacher, and has developed several isometric (60°) triangle rulers. Sara's quilting career has taken her all over the United States, Canada and Australia. Her quilts have been exhibited in many places. She has been featured in magazine articles, and her quilts have been in books by other authors.

Milwaukee, Wisconsin is the birth place of Sara Nephew, where she grew up and went to high school and college as an art major. She started her career as a commercial jeweler and began to learn diamond setting, as well as continuing her work with painting and cloisonné enameling.

Sara married Dale and moved to Seattle, Washington where Dale worked for Boeing. Sara continued to work at home, making original design cloisonné and gold and silver jewelry, selling her work at art fairs and by word of mouth. The couple eventually bought three acres in the country in an area called Clearview, north of Seattle. Sara planted vegetable gardens, raised chickens, ducks, geese, and turkeys, milled her own grain and baked bread from scratch, even made her own soap. Quilting seemed like another "country" kind of thing to do, as well as a way to economically decorate their nineteen thirties-built home. With three little children, quilting, with a sewing machine and lots of beautiful fabric, seemed much more child-friendly than a jeweler's torches, kilns, and acid. She joined the local guild and began quilting.

Clearview Triangle is the business Sara started as her multifaceted quilting career took off. But in 2006 Sara retired from the day to day operation of running her business and sold her company, Clearview Triangle, to Marci Baker of Alicia's Attic. However, Sara Nephew has not stopped working, creating new quilts, or writing books, as evidenced by this book. Sara's latest title merges into Marci's series of "Not Your Grandmother's Quilts". It is spectacular!

Contact her at saranephew@aliciasattic.com.

*Mexican Star, right, 55" x 62", features a decorator fabric border print (found at a garage sale) that surrounds the almost iridescent colors in the log cabin star. Burgeoning floral motifs contrast with geometric blocks and strips. This quilt swirls with texture. Judy followed the flowers and leaves with her quilting, adding to the rich detail of the design. Pieced by Sara Nephew and machine quilted by Judy Irish.*

# Marci Baker

Recognized internationally for her expertise in quilting, Marci enjoys sharing ideas that simplify the process of quilting. A native of Dallas, Texas, Marci has loved sewing for years, making her first quilt at age 9 and sewing her own clothes in high school and college. She began teaching quilting in 1989 for her local quilting guild and shops. Marci graduated with a bachelor's and master's degree in math. In 1993 she started Alicia's Attic with the concepts that combine her love of math with her love of quilting. Quilting became a great way to share her knowledge with others.

As an admirer of traditional quilts, Marci was inspired to author books on "Not Your Grandmother's™ Quilts". This series uses the traditional patterns people associate with their grandmother and simplifies the technique. She has invented several tools to help make quilting easier for all. Her Know Before You Sew™ solution cards take common problems quilters encounter, and provide easy-to-understand solutions.

Marci spends much of the year traveling, teaching classes for quilting guilds and trade shows. Enthusiasm and inspiration for quilting can be seen throughout her lectures, workshops, and books. She has been featured in Redbook, on Home and Garden TV's "Simply Quilts", Quilters' News Network, NBC's "The Jane Pauley Show", highlighted in "Traditional Quiltworks", and has been published in numerous quilting magazines. Marci has been nominated for The Professional Quilter magazine "Teacher of the Year" award in 2002 and 2005.

In 2006 she expanded Alicia's Attic by purchasing Clearview Triangle from Sara Nephew. They are collaborating on new designs and techniques to inspire today's quilter.

Marci and her husband Clint, their sons, Kevin and Marcus, and the family pet snake, Scooby, currently live in Fort Collins, Colorado where they enjoy the outdoors and the beautiful creation of life near the mountains.

Contact her at marcibaker@aliciasattic.com.